Heaven and Earth
As One

Book II in the Heaven's Chambers series

Jamie L. Wilson

www.HeavensChambers.com

Wilson House Publishing

Asheville North Carolina

Unless otherwise indicated, all Scripture quotations are taken from the *Holy Bible, New living Translation,* copyright © 1996, 2004, 2015 by Tyndale House Foundation, used by permission of Tyndale House Publishers, Inc., Carol Stream, Illinois 60188. All rights reserved. Scripture quotations marked (NASB) are taken from the New American Standard Bible, copyright © 1960, 1962, 1963, 1971, 1972, 1973, 1975, 1977, 1955 by the Lockman Foundation. Used by permission. Scripture quotations marked (RSV) are taken from the Revised Standard Version of the Holy Bible, copyright © 1952 (2nd edition, 1971) by the division of Christ in the United States of America, Used by permission. Scripture quotations marked (NIV) are from the Holy Bible, New International Version copyright © 1973, 1978, 1984, 2011 by Biblica. All rights reserved worldwide. Used by permission. Scripture quotations marked (ESV) are from the Holy Bible, English Standard Version, copyright © 2001 by Crossway Bibles, a division of Good News Publishers. Used by permission. Scripture quotations marked (KJB) are from the Bible (public domain in America) 1611 King James Bible 'Authorized Version' of the King James Bible (Pure Cambridge edition). Used by Permission. Scripture quotations marked (NKJV) are taken from the New King James Version copyright © 1982 by Thomas Nelson. Used by permission. All rights reserved.

➢ Please take note that Wilson House Publishing does not capitalize the name satan, except when beginning a sentence, which may differ from other publisher's styles and even breaks grammatical rules. We simply choose not to give him any form of respect.

Publishers Information:

Wilson House Publishing

Asheville North Carolina

info@wilsonhousepublishing.com

www.wilsonhousepublishing.com

ISBN Number 978-0-9888076-4-8

Available through the publisher's website, the author's website, and online stores like Amazon in paperback or e-book format or through your local book store.

➢ Cover photograph-Bryan Cooper

Introduction

Jesus is always active in a believer's life, that is if we allow Him to be. And if we do, you and I will accomplish more than we could ever imagine! I knew I was supposed to write three books, but I never imagined the Lord would ask me to continue to write a series of books. Jesus has revealed to me that He will never stop giving me New assignments to complete. He will continue to speak His New Revelations to me as I continue to go up and into my chamber in heaven to be with Him. After all, He did custom build this dwelling place especially for me just like He has built one for all His children. What that means is that the books in my Heaven's Chambers series will continue even beyond the three and that is perfectly fine with me. It is you, Lord, who placed this gifting inside of me. It is you who gave me a place to start by inspiring me to keep writing in my journals. You sparked a revelation from one of my journals that became my first book and now I can write to my heart's content. "I *will praise you, O Lord with all my heart; I will tell of all your Wonders."* Psalm 9:1 (NIV) This bible verse is what my books are all about. My heart thanks you Father, Son, and Holy Spirit. Together we write!

Table of Contents

One

Again Chamber

Here we go again! Jesus and I on this roller coaster ride. And the best part is... we are riding it together right up to Heaven and back down to earth. I love the many new twist and turns we are taking on this ride and what incredible fun we are having! I have found that these New Heavenly Chamber meetings have increased as New thoughts, New knowledge, New ideas and New insights have accelerated as Jesus draws me up and in again and deeper into Himself. Drawing me right up and into the center of His heart.

Every morning I wake up, I open my eyes, I look up while my head is resting in comfort on my soft pillow, and I see floating in the air right in front of my eyes what appears to be pieces of DNA. It's as if I am looking at them under a microscope. I can literally see the DNA of heaven floating in the air. I actually see them! Regardless of where I may be, whether I am indoors or outdoors, they are visible for me to see. Why is this? Because the air of heaven is all around me, all around us. We live in it and we breathe it in.

My husband Jay and our daughter Tanique see them too! And do you know what? You Can Too! Do you remember the popular worship song by Michael W. Smith, "This is the Air I Breathe"? This song reminds me that Jesus is the very air we breathe! He is our breath of life! Jesus can clearly give to you, as He has given to me, the clear vision to see the air of Heaven as it invades and mingles in with the air we breathe right here on the earth. Heaven's air literally becomes visible for us to see!

One morning in 2013 while I was sitting on my bed, I went up and into my chamber to be with Jesus and He Himself taught me how to gaze up and look into the air, how to wait for it and how to see more of it. All I did was listen to His directions. I obeyed Him and then they started to simply appear "one by one." I began to see them appear and when I did, I started sketching them down the best I could in my journal. These tiny pieces of matter, these substances, each have their own unique shape, design and size and they are a warm light glowing color.

I will only explain to you what some of them look like because every day I see new ones appear. Some resemble a thread like substance which look to be only a few centimeters in length. They remind me of a thin piece of thread that a seamstress uses to sew. They look similar to the shape between these parenthesis (/).

I will often see these thread-like strands floating as a single piece of thread all by themselves while other single pieces of thread will gather together to make up a set of three threads. The set of three will be floating inside a clear circular shape. I also see sets of three strands similar to these (///) floating inside of an oblong shape that glows with a light white color. The oblong shape seems to be filled with a clear liquid. Many of these oblong shapes hold three separate sets of three strands and these three sets will be perfectly spaced between each other as if they are standing side by side. The total number of strands in one oblong shape equals nine strands in all and the number nine in the bible also refers to finality and completeness.

Another single thread like strand I see is thicker in width and has a wispy slight curve shape to it which measures about one-fourth of an inch in length resembling something like a feather. While others look like a small clear circle. Again, I will give you a similar example by typing the circle size inside of these parenthesis (o).

Each small circle is a clear round globe that is outlined with a black color and is filled with living light and the light has movement and is alive. While other clear looking circles will contain one small glowing dot floating in the middle of them and the color of the dot is a mixture of gray and black. The glowing dot contains a watery substance which also has movement in it like the waves of an ocean.

It is so amazing to view all these pieces of matter. God commands the speed of each of them as they dance in a synchronized dance in the air. Each one contains a piece of God's life in them. I believe it is His DNA and Jay refers to them as the essence of Heaven.

Each one will slowly fall or swirl and twirl around me in a circular pattern of movement and as I look upward new ones appear. They too will float down around me or on me. I like to extend out my hand, or at times both of my hands, and catch them one by one as they settle on either palm. Whenever Lola, my little Chihuahua, would be sitting with me on my bed they would settle on the back of her neck and she would move in enjoyment as if I were petting her. What a wonderful realm our Father lives in.

We do not have to wait for these experiences until we go home to Heaven. We can experience countless glimpses of Heaven every day by just existing in His air we breathe. We are alive because God breathed his breath of life into us, His creation. When we breathe Him in, we live *forever*. God's Holy Spirit is our Breath of Life!

Did you know the Hebrew word for spirit is Ruach and its meaning is "air in motion?" And Ruach is the same word spoken for the meaning of the word "breath" and also for the word "life." Three meanings in one Hebrew word (breath, life, and air in motion) or (breath, wind, and spirit). No wonder the spoken word of God sets everything into motion. Life began when He breathed His breath of life into all of His creation!

"Then the Lord God formed the man of dust from the ground and breathed into his nostrils the breath of life; and the man became a living being." Genesis 2:7 (RSV)

"As long as my breath is in me, and the spirit of God is in my nostrils." Job 27:3 (ESV)

"If He should set His heart to it and gather to Himself His spirit and His breath, all flesh would perish together, and man would return to dust." Job 34:14-15 (ESV)

"And when He had said this, He breathed on them and said to them, "Receive the Holy Spirit." John 20:22 (ESV)

Two

Listen Chamber

Keep on Keeping

"Keep listening my little one, for if you do then all will be well, all will be plentiful for all is mine. I choose to give you my all." These words Jesus personally shared with me while I was up and in the *Listen Chamber* with Him.

The first word He spoke to me is the word "Keep." This word "Keep" is a vital key to unlocking my door to obedience as I keep listening to the Holy Spirit and keep fulfilling all the assignments He gives to me. Listening keeps my door unlocked and my heart open so I will continually be filled with His spirit of obedience. As I keep being filled, I keep being obedient. It's really quite simple to do. I find obedience is nothing but **fun.** I "Keep on Keeping" because when I choose to apply this key action word it is the first key, the first turning point in allowing myself to be an obedient servant; a servant open to receiving the gift of obedience from Jesus who is God's obedient son. In obedience, we believers will boldly walk right into God's open doors, His doors placed before us. Doors that are spiritually open in heaven and on earth as well.

Jesus will continue to teach us the keys of His Holy Words, spoken directly from Him or as we read them in His Holy Bible. His key words are kept inside us and each key word can be inserted to unlock our ears to keep listening, to unlock our hearts, to keep staying open, to keep believing, to keep receiving, and to keep obeying. Then we will be unlocked with open arms, open lives, and especially open ears giving us the ability to "Keep on Keeping" open to Him.

His listening keys will tell us which key opens which door. All these keys are to be kept deep inside our hearts, locked up safe and secure! They are to be kept there until one key is to be taken out and inserted to open a specific door that stands before us on earth and in heaven. We simply gain entrance by walking through the open door. I believe we must keep living our lives to simply LISTEN, to simply OBEY, and to keep inserting our keys to either open or shut doors in both realms, Heaven and Earth. If we love Him, we will obey Him and if we obey Him it is because we Love Him.

Look for Key Words in These Scriptures

James 1:19-22 *"My dear brothers and sisters, be quick to listen, slow to speak, and slow to get angry. Your anger can never make things right in God's sight. So get rid of all the filth and evil in your lives, and humbly accept the message God has planted in your hearts, for it is strong enough to save your souls."*

Judges 2:17 *"Yet Israel did not listen to the judges but prostituted themselves to other gods, bowing down to them. How quickly they turned away from the path of their ancestors, who had walked in obedience to the Lord's commands."*

Genesis 6:16 *"Make a roof for it and finish the ark to within 18 inches of the top. Put a door in the side of the ark and make lower, middle and upper decks."*

Revelation 1:18 *"I am the living one who died. Look, I am alive forever and ever! And I hold the keys of death and the grave."*

Matthew 16:19 *"And I will give you the keys of the Kingdom of Heaven. Whatever you lock on earth will be locked in heaven, and whatever you open on earth will be opened in heaven."*

Three

Silence Chamber

In the *silence* I can hear Him! This word silence is also a very important key word to activate whenever we go up and into our chamber. Our entire being must be silent. Why? The answer is found here in Job 33:31-33 (NASB) *"Pay attention, O Job, listen to me; keep silent, and let me speak. Then if you have anything to say, answer me; speak, for I desire to justify you. If not, listen to me; keep silent, and I will teach you wisdom."* There is that unlocking key word again, "KEEP." The Father is telling us how to obey. We are to listen by Keeping Silent. These verses are sure an attention getter for me. Are they for you?

The Father desires to teach us but He wants our full undivided attention. He wants us *one on one* with Him in our very own Chamber to teach us Wisdom! Job 13:5 (NASB) *"O that you would be completely silent, and that it would become your wisdom!"* I believe from my times with Him, in my Silence Chamber, my Father is not only about a one-way conversation where He does all the talking or where we do all the talking. He wants desperately to have a two-way conversation with us, His children.

I remember a time when I had rushed into my Chamber. I must admit that I was impatient as I waited for Jesus to come to be with me and as soon as His glorious presence entered, I started to talk like a Chatty Cathy doll.

I don't know if you are familiar with this doll but when I was young this was a new doll on the market. You pulled the string on the back of the doll until it was completely out and then you would release the string. The doll would talk, repeating the same few phrases. The doll would talk with quick chattering words. Today, the Chatty Cathy doll is considered a vintage doll.

Well, I was chatting like this doll as if a person just kept pulling my string over and over again without ever taking a break. I remember I was rambling on and on and on. I finally paused a second to catch my breath. As I did, I looked at Jesus. He was standing there with His right index finger touching His lips and I heard him make a soft but very loving Shh sound. I then realized I had taken over the entire conversation. Jesus smiled at me. His smile and quiet Shh reminded me to quiet down my voice and my whole being and be silent so I could be taught wisdom from my Jesus.

Whenever we go up and into our Chambers, it is important to relax and to set our thoughts aside, to not worry and to not fret. We need to leave our cares, so to speak, down here on the earth because we are actually traveling *spiritually* up to the Heavens to wait and to meet with Jesus in our very own private chamber dwelling place. *"How lovely is your dwelling place O Lord Almighty"* Psalm 84:1. It's a dwelling place that He built and prepared for each one of us to come into. A chamber which is free from any earthly distractions and we can stay and dwell with our Lord and Savior as long as our heart desires.

I believe that is a vital lesson to learn; when to be silent and when to speak all the while we are on this earth, living our lives in Christ and expanding His Kingdom His Way. It's especially important now as the evil one seems to be working overtime as we, The Brides of Christ, rise up and conquer our own territories. I believe it is important to ask God which land of promise He has chosen for you to live in. If you are already in your land of promise then stay. If you are not there, ask Him where He would like you to go, He will tell you. Let us choose to stay obedient and open to receive all the new garments of wisdom the Lord desires to place around us. We are robed in His love and righteousness as we move forward. Isaiah

61:10 (RSV) *"I will greatly rejoice in the Lord, my soul shall exult in my God; for He has clothed me with the garments of salvation, He has covered me with the robe of righteousness, as a bridegroom decks himself with a garland, and as a bride adorns herself with her jewels."*

Here are a few scriptures to remind us when to keep silent......

Proverbs 10:19 (NASB) *"When there are many words, transgression is unavoidable, but he who restrains his lips is wise."*

Proverbs 11:12 (NASB) *"He who despises his neighbor lacks sense, but a man of understanding keeps silent."*

Ecclesiastes 3:7 (KJB) *"A time to rend, and a time to sew; a time to keep silent, and a time to speak."*

Four

Rejoice Chamber

"This is the day that the Lord has made I will rejoice and be glad in it!"

I have one sister who is a year older than me. Her name is Penny. She would often quote to me from Psalm 118:24. In this Psalm it tells us that we are to be glad in the days we are given. This is a proclamation to herself in honor of God while in the midst of her physical pain.

I would like to share with you the old life my sister lived that she no longer lives today because God is faithful and her healing has begun! My sister had been ill for 20 years or longer. One morning years ago she woke up with flu symptoms which never seemed to go away. Instead, these flu symptoms continued to increase throughout the years causing her to spend her days bed ridden.

I remember her tearful phone calls to me as it took every ounce of energy inside of her to ask me to pray for her. My heart felt her words of pain and suffering as we would pray together.

I love my sister and Jesus loves her far more than I could ever comprehend. Jesus also suffered tremendous pain and agony on that day of crucifixion so very long ago. But in the midst of pain, He rejoiced. Just as the one hanging next to Him did when Jesus turned to him and said, *"I assure you today, you will be with me in paradise!"* Luke 23:43. Only the **love** of Jesus will heal our pain, our sorrows, and our suffering. Only in His timing, only in His way, only by His love can we rejoice and say, "This is the day that the Lord has made, we will rejoice and be glad in it!"

We all experience painful days, never forget Jesus did too! Let us never forget what His love conquered and what His love is. He is the healer who loves us right through the pain. His love will bring us right into complete and total healing. His love will end our suffering and His love will bring restoration into our lives this very day. I will write a prayer for you to speak out loud and while you pray you may feel enemy spirits stirring inside of you. Take deep breaths and cough to expel these intruders and then continue to speak out the prayer, cough deeply and Jesus will help guide you, He is with you.

Father, in the name of Jesus and by the healing blood of the lamb, I ask you to command the enemy to loosen every physical ailment, every spirit of infirmity, and all those under or above its kingdom, to be bound together with God's triple braided cord and to be sent out from within me. Jesus break all the past and present curses from my mother and father's bloodlines and keep my future generations cleansed. Send in your hosts to completely cut, with the sword of the Spirit, and pull out all these evil spirits, their roots, darts, hooks, fetters and arrows which have been placed inside my heart, soul, mind, organs and body. In Jesus name, I command every evil spirit to go to Jesus and to get out of me right now! In Jesus name, I command these spirits to never replace themselves or return to me for I am a beautiful child of God. Jesus reverse all the damage and all the pain that each one of these spirits have caused me. Pour into me your anointed healing power and restore me, your child, to wholeness. Jesus rise up in me your fire of love. Let your anointed healing oil flow and fill every cell within my heart, my soul, my mind, my organs and my body. I praise you, I thank you, and I will live for you, forever. Amen.

Isaiah 57:19 *"Then words of praise will be on their lips. May they have peace, both near and far, for I will heal them all, says the Lord."*

Lift up Mountains

Our God is very awesome in how and when He decides to display His gift of healing through us, His bridal vessels. I believe a Glorious day is coming *soon* where the brides will speak healing words out loud to the one they see in need. That need will be filled because the word of the Lord was spoken in authority to heal each one of them. Joshua 21:45 (NKJV) *"Not a word failed of any good thing which the Lord had spoken to the house of Israel. All came to pass."*

I was driving my car through downtown Hendersonville, North Carolina on a beautiful summer day in 2012. I had decided to run some errands. As I was driving slowly, I saw a middle-aged woman who was limping as she walked along the sidewalk. I noticed from the expression on her face that she was in considerable pain with each step she took.

I immediately felt great love and compassion for this woman. The Holy Spirit started to stir and churn inside of me. The churning reminded me of a tornado. I felt the power rising up through me and I could feel a mighty whirlwind of healing words bursting up from deep within my being and out of my mouth. I was shouting at the top of my lungs but everything was in perfect control. As I continued to drive past this woman, I kept speaking healing words out loud.

As I watched her walk, she limped from obvious pain

with each step she took. The Holy Spirit proclaimed words to her that one of her next steps would be without a limp. I continued to slowly drive past this woman and as I did I kept my eye on her in my rear-view mirror and kept speaking out the Holy Spirit's words to heal her.

Sure enough, the limp became increasingly less and less with each step she took. I knew that I knew that I knew by the time she reached her destination she would limp no more! That is exactly what happened. Believe it when you speak it!

People of God, it takes the faith as tiny as a mustard seed to say to this mountain, "be thrown into the sea," and it will obey you! I don't know about you but I am going out to see how many mountains I can throw into the sea through my faith. I threw one into the sea with this woman and I have named it Limp Mountain!

Mark 11:23 (NIV) *"Truly I tell you, if anyone says to* **this mountain,** *'Go,* **throw** *yourself* **into** *the* **sea,** *' and does not doubt in their heart but believes that what they say will happen, it will be done for them."*

Hebrews 11:1 *"What is faith? It is the confident assurance that what we hope for is going to happen. It is the evidence of things we cannot yet see."*

Five

Healing Chamber

Healing belongs to our God and **not** to the enemy. *"I am the Lord who heals you."* Exodus 15:26 (NIV) I love the promise of healing we find in Jeremiah 30:17 *"I will give you back your health and heal your wounds, says the Lord."*

I love being up and in the healing chamber with Jesus. Often, He will discuss with me a brand-new healing assignment that he would like me to go on. Most of the time He will ask me to go at a moment's notice or in a few hours or in a few days.

Jay and I have decided to be on Jesus' time table and not on our own. Jesus is the first one we love. Jesus is the first one we love to obey. Jesus is the wise one who tells Jay and I the new comings and goings He would like us to participate in. He doesn't always give us *all* the details. Often He will say go here or go there.

When we arrive at our destination, He directs us where we are to sit and wait for the person or the opportunity we are to engage in.

Jesus will tell me when I am to go alone or when Jay or Tanique are to join me. The awesome part is, Jesus will always tell each one of us when we are to join together or when to go alone. I look at it as being the obedient Bride of Christ, a bride who will always listen in the spirit and be ready to go at a moment's notice. Every time the command is given to go, the bride must go!

Let me share with you a few of our healing adventures. One morning in early summer in 2012, I was in my chamber and Jesus asked me to go on a two-hour drive from our home in Asheville to a place located in a township called Moravian Falls, North Carolina. I called Jay at his office to tell him and sure enough Jesus had already begun to stir in Jay's heart the same thing. Two days later, Saturday, we drove the two hours to where a small waterfall is located on the property of a privately-owned campground called Moravian Falls Family Campground.

The owners who are believers allow the public to come and sit at their waterfall without needing a camping reservation. When we arrived, we parked our car and checked in at the camp office. We walked a short distance across the small unpaved parking lot to a grassy area beneath the falls. This area had a few picnic tables that were spread out so people could sit on them to view this small, beautiful waterfall. We were to simply go and sit at the picnic table the Lord chose for us and patiently wait for the *one* Jesus would send to us.

This waterfall is a popular place here in North Carolina, especially within the Christian community. Believers of all ages love to come and sit by this beautiful waterfall to seek out God, to worship Him in purity and in truth and wait to hear from Him. Many receive New vision and divine direction for their lives or in their ministries. Psalm 46:3 *"Let the oceans roar and foam. Let the Mountains tremble as the waters surge!"*

This was the first time we traveled to Moravian Falls to experience the gentle surge of water cascading from this beautiful waterfall and bask in God's presence there. We were very excited because this place had been on our agenda of places to visit during our first few years living in North Carolina. As Jay and I sat, we noticed a few people standing around but our focus drifted toward a blond-haired woman who was reading her bible. She sat across the narrow stream from us.

After we had been sitting by the waterfall for about 20 minutes a woman who was wearing a bright yellow t-shirt, and looked to be in her late 30's, came walking to our picnic table. We realized she was the blond-haired woman who had been sitting across the stream from us. Jay and I both looked at the woman then at each other and at the same time we said, "This is the one."

The Lord asked me to get up and to greet her with a handshake. She stood by our picnic table looking at us as she introduced herself. She said, "Did the Lord tell you to come here and wait?" Jay and I both laughed and said, "Yes He did." She said, "Me too."

We told each other our names and began to hug each other before we all sat down at the picnic table. She sat directly across from me while Jay sat to my right. We began to share our stories with each other about how Jesus led each one of us here to Moravian Falls on this particular Saturday. It did not take Jay and I long to discern the reason why the Lord had brought us here. We were sent here to battle spiritually for this woman.

She was a single mom, raising her daughter alone. She spoke with despair in her voice as she told us how she desired to have more of the love, encouragement, and blood power of Jesus in her life to free her from an occult spirit. This occult spirit (spirit guide) came into her life years before. It happened when she was involved in the New Age movement. The spirit guide was still invading her dreams and hampering her walk with the Lord.

She began to tell us how she innocently fell into

the New Age movement and how her involvement grew to the point where she had been trained by a spirit guide to be a reiki healer. (Note: satan is the one who is in control of reiki healing. The enemy can cause the infirmity in the person and then also remove or hide it so the person believes the reiki healer was the healer. A reiki healer places their hands lightly on or over the person's body to facilitate the healing. It is considered a type of therapy.) This woman shared that she had healed many people while she was a reiki healer in the New Age movement. She began to tell us that three years prior she wanted to get out of this occult but her spirit guide would not allow her to leave.

The spirit guide caused severe pain in her back which became so extreme that she sought out medical help. She was prescribed pain medication to cope with her back pain. I felt such hurt for this woman and knew that I needed to place both of my hands on top of her hands while she had them resting on the picnic table in front of her. I couldn't stop looking into her eyes.

She continued to tell Jay and I that she had been standing at the counter in her kitchen one day. She was looking at the bottle of pain medication and telling herself the only way to end this unbearable pain was to over dose on her pain medication. As she started to reach for the bottle a memory started to rise up within herself. She began to remember back in time to when she was a young girl and remembered the Jesus of her childhood. The severe pain continued to worsen inside her lower back until she collapsed to the kitchen floor. She lay crying and screaming for this evil to leave her alone. She didn't know what to do or how to stop this demonic spirit guide from stabbing her!

As she was screaming out in pain something started to rise up from deep within her. Her childhood memory of Jesus as her savior began to take over and increase inside of her. She could feel and hear her screams being transformed into power and with her mouth she cried out, Jesus, Jesus, Jesus, over and over and over again! Her cry was heard in Heaven! Psalm 18:6 *"But in my distress I cried out to the Lord; Yes, I prayed to my God for help. He heard me from His sanctuary; my cry reached His ears."*

Jesus heard the heart of a child crying and when she screamed for Him, He came to save her. He touched her and the pain left. Her childhood memory rose up in her and gave her the heart of a child who cried out to Jesus for help and He rescued her. He brought her back into a right relationship with the Father, Son and Holy Spirit. She was born again in His love. Romans 10:9 *"For if you confess with your mouth that Jesus is Lord and believe in your heart that God raised Him from the dead, you will be saved."*

When she had finished telling us her experience I

said to her, "Would you like to get rid of this spirit guide for good, right now?" Words cannot express the look of hope that lit up her face. Immediately she responded with, "Yes!" So, with the guidance of the Holy Spirit the three of us held hands together while sitting on the benches of the picnic table. We could hear the gentle surge of the water cascading down the waterfall and feel the warmth of the sun.

I love going to Jesus *first* for direction and for protection whenever engaging in a battle against evil. In this case the Lord sent Michael, God's Archangel, to join us. (See Jude 1:9 & Revelation 12:7-8.) He came with plenty of Hosts to help us battle for her release. I remember seeing Michael and three rows deep of mighty battle angels all lined up. They all stood in perfect alignment a short distance behind this woman. We felt surrounded with the Glory of God!

The occult spirit and his kingdom were outnumbered so the battle was quick, and in no time this woman was glowing with freedom. Philippians 2:10 *"So that at the name of Jesus every knee will bow, in heaven and on the earth and under the earth."*

Jay and I had the honor to share other truths with her as we continued to encourage her to simply go to Jesus *first*. He will train her daily in her heavenly chamber. It is in this place she will learn how to maintain her freedom and her healing, just like all of us can.

As we were rejoicing in the Lord the three of us noticed two women walking toward us. One looked to be middle-aged and the other in her early twenties. Both of them had a look of bewilderment on their faces as they approached our picnic table. Our new friend stood to greet them exactly like the greeting we had with her. She asked them, "Did the Lord tell you to come here and wait?"

You should have seen the look on their faces as they both said, "Yes" and the three of us said, "Us too!" Then, with a great deal of laughter and hugs to go around they sat down with us at the picnic table as well. The woman introduced herself and her daughter and then began to tell the three of us their story.

Jesus had asked this woman two days prior to come here to Moravian Falls to this waterfall at this campground on this Saturday and to simply wait. After she heard His request the woman shared it with her daughter. Her daughter shared with us that she had recently recommitted her life to Jesus and felt led to come along also.

Neither one of them had heard of Moravian Falls nor did they know if it was an actual place. They immediately began to search the internet and were excited to see that Moravian Falls Family Campground and Moravian falls did exist, but it was a considerable distance from their home state so driving was not going to be an option for them. The woman called an airline to book a flight for herself and her daughter so they would arrive on Saturday but the cost for two plane tickets was more than they could afford. They decided to tell God that if He wanted them in Moravian Falls He would need to send a miracle.

The next day, which was Friday, she received a phone call from the airline and the gentleman on the phone said, "Your name is on our ticket waiting list, would you like to book your ticket reservations to North Carolina? The cost will be one hundred dollars per ticket." The woman said, "What are you talking about I never asked to be put on this list." The gentleman said, "Yes, you did!"

He again repeated her name as he read it off to her from the waiting list and asked, "Do you want the tickets?" She then realized this was the miracle she asked Jesus for and quickly said, "Yes!" God also made sure that there was an open reservation in one of the cabins at the campground for them to stay in. It was such a joy as we sat on the picnic table and continued to tell each other the details of our stories.

This woman and her daughter were led by the Holy Spirit to bring along some crackers and juice to share in communion and they asked us to join them. The crackers and juice were blessed before being served and the special feeling of unity was drawing us into the glory of God as we gathered together as the body of Christ. We ended our time together with a lasting memory of the mother and her daughter lying in the shallow water just below the gentle surging water of Moravian Falls with their eyes looking up to Heaven while they experienced their own individual water baptism. It was as if they were laying before the throne of God. He was looking down on them as the sun slowly began to bring an end to this glorious day. Psalm 121:1-2, *"I look up to the mountains--- does my help come from there? My help comes from the Lord, who made the heavens and the earth!"*

Six

Open Chamber

I love choosing to be an open vessel for the Lord, to flow His supernatural miracle power through me whenever He chooses. I love being taught by Jesus in my open chamber. He is my own private teacher. He teaches me how to release His gift of working miracles through me to bring Him all the glory. I listen intently to His lessons every time I go up and into my open chamber. I eagerly sit down in His class room to absorb His words as He teaches me and I take notes.

I personally believe, because of my own one on one experiences with Jesus, that we believers need to aggressively seek the face of Jesus first and foremost like this verse encourages us to do in Psalm 27:8 (ESV) *"You have said, "Seek my face," My heart says to you, "Your face, Lord, do I seek."* It is our hearts telling us to seek the face of our Lord.

I have seen the face of our Lord Jesus Christ many times in my chamber in heaven and I continue to see Him appear to me in the physical and in spiritual manifestations here on earth. When I least expect it, He suddenly appears! John 20:19 *"Suddenly, Jesus was standing there among them!"* This is how it is for me, Jesus will be standing there unexpectedly.

It happened in the first house we were renting in Western North Carolina. It was ten o'clock in the evening and the early part of summer, 2013. I walked to the back of our home to close the double glass sliding doors which led out to the sun-room just steps away from the kitchen. The kitchen and sun-room lights were turned off but I did have a light on in our front hallway that was giving off sufficient light to see where I was walking. The kitchen, dining room, living room, and hallway were open concept. All these rooms were able to be seen while standing in the back of our home.

When I finished closing the glass door, I began to turn around with the mindset of going to bed. It had been a long day and I was tired. As I turned to take my first step, I decided to glance over to my right and look into the kitchen. I could see a tall man standing in the middle of the dimly lit kitchen. I knew without a doubt who this man was as I gazed right into His eyes. It was a very familiar face. It was Jesus.

Jesus has the most beautiful smile that lights up

the entire room. His eyes are a beautiful azure. They are eternal pools filled with pure love that pulls me in deeper and deeper until my entire being seems to stand naked before him. I know I am clothed in His righteousness and in His love while I am being swaddled up in a Heavenly blanket of His blue majestic eyes. Isaiah 43:4 (ESV) *"you are precious in my eyes...and I love you."*

While it felt like an eternity, it was only a few seconds before I continued down the hallway and to bed for the evening. I know who my Jesus is so I am never afraid or startled when He decides to show Himself to me. His presence is all love. Fear can not exist in His presence.

This was not the first time Jesus had appeared to me as a man. A few weeks prior Jesus appeared to me as a tall, suntanned gardener with black wavy shoulder length hair. He was wearing a beige straw woven hat on his head that looked to me like it had been hand made by someone living on a tropical island selling them to tourists. Jesus was also wearing a white cotton shirt; light tan work pants and He carried a weed eater in His right hand.

I remember the handle of the weed eater was black and the base of it was a deep red color. I watched Him from my bedroom window as He walked up our neighbor's steep driveway across the road from our home. He continued to walk at a slow pace and walked right up to our neighbor's front door and walked right through it. Mark 16:12 (NIV) *"Afterward Jesus appeared in a different form to two of them while they were walking in the country."*

Let's get back to after I saw Jesus in my kitchen. I had put on my comfortable PJs and crawled into bed. I was starting to doze off when Jesus appeared once again! He was standing to the right side of my bed and this time He was in a spiritual form, full of light. I could see his outline. The outline looked like the man who had been standing in my kitchen moments prior.

I stared at Him for a while before I whispered, "I know who you are." Jesus replied back with a whisper, "Yes, you know who I am." I continued to gaze at Jesus and again in a whisper asked, "Why did you come to see me?" He whispered, "To tell you how much I love you!" We spent about an hour and a half whispering back and forth saying how much we loved each other. At the end, He said, "I am going to leave now," so I said my goodbye. Jesus appeared in love and He left in love. He is love and I could still see His glow lingering after He left. I was still gazing at it as I drifted off to sleep.

It doesn't end there because every day I go up and into my chamber to wait on Him, to be with Him, to talk with Him. I see Jesus every day. His face, eyes, and smile are always the same and I can recognize Him anywhere! Jesus is my Savior, my daddy, my deliverer, my mentor. He is the lover of my soul. I also know who my God in heaven is. He is pure love. He is the one who sits upon His throne. He is my Father, my dad. He is bigger than life and He keeps me safe in His arms as I often sit upon his lap!

I even know who my Holy Spirit is. I am filled with His tremendous love and power. He is my Friend. He teaches me truth and always tells me what's up! The Holy Spirit and I will travel in the spirit together. We spirit travel inside His lightning bolt. He will take me to the past, to the future, or we soar in the heavens in the present. My Holy Spirit will always hold on to my left arm above my elbow with a strong but gentle grip before we take off and fly.

Lately, He has been teaching me that I can ask Him to take me anywhere I want to go. If I go someplace I want it to be purposeful though. It has to have a purpose like snatching people from hell. I often joke with my mom and sister saying, "Don't be surprised if one day I show up in your kitchen."

All three persons of the trinity are my BFFs. I personally know them. They each have a great sense of humor and make me laugh all the time. Tears of laughter are the best tears to cry. The three in one are my Everything! I love them! I know what each one looks like. All three of them have the form of a man. Genesis 1:26 (KJB) refers to this saying, "*let us make man in our image, after our likeness."* The word *our* in this verse is referring to God, Jesus and Holy Spirit.

God is gigantic as He sits upon His throne. He radiates with glorious white and colorful lights. I like how His white glistening hair is somewhat long and flows with a life of its own. Jesus is around 6 feet tall. He is strong in stature, has exquisite blue eyes and a glistening smile. I know now that Jesus has wings, but I have never seen them. God also reveals this to us in Psalm 91:4, Psalm 17:8 and Ruth 2:12. Jesus is beautiful beyond description.

Spring of 2018 was the first time my eyes were opened to get a quick look to see the image of what the Holy Spirit looks like although we had traveled together many times before. He has the form of a man similar to Jesus. His hair is beautiful and quite long. He's extremely muscular, buffed, yet very gentle. This gentleness reminds me of how a mother will lovingly hold her new born baby in her arms. But, I feel He is the most mysterious. He radiates "glowing-glory power." He travels at the speed of light, like the flash of a white lightning bolt in the sky. He is purity and is consumed with truth and wisdom. He likes to talk to me a lot and I like talking to Him.

God, Jesus and Holy Spirit will talk with me throughout my day and often late into the evening. One thing I know for sure is if I can know and see the

Father, the Son and the Holy Spirt, and can travel with them, so can all of His children!

"He showed you these things so you would realize that the Lord is God and that there is no other god." Deuteronomy 4:35

"Now stand up! For I have appeared to you to appoint you as my servant and my witness. You are to tell the world about this experience and about other times I will appear to you." Acts 26:16

"The Spirit lifted me up and took me away." Ezekiel 3:14

Streets of Golden Opportunity

Jay and I live in Asheville, North Carolina and we love to walk up and down the maze of sidewalks that make up the streets of downtown. As we casually stroll these streets, we love to watch the people and become a part of all the activity around us. There are a variety of musical instruments being played and many songs being sung as people stand or sit on a street corner or in front of the many endless array of coffee and eclectic shops.

The Holy Spirit will always guide Jay and I while we walk on these streets of golden opportunity. Strategically, He will lead us into an open street opportunity to have conversation with someone. We enjoy asking people questions about what is important to them. Before you know it, God has opened up a place in our conversation for us to talk to them about who He is in our lives. This is easy for us because Jesus is our life and He is always on our minds. His name naturally comes up in our conversations. We don't have to think about it or rehearse any kind of a script before conversing with anyone.

Let me tell you about something that is continually being said as we converse with people. The comment we hear from individuals over and over and over again is, "I used to go to church" or "I should go to church." Our response is always the same, "He loves you for you. Jesus wants to have a *one on one* friendship with you. Why? Because He loves you right now, right where you are whether you go to church or not. He died because of His love for you!"

Often, we see a look of confusion on their faces when they are told they are loved by Jesus despite the fact they don't go to church. They look at us baffled, and in disbelief wondering why Jesus loves them when they haven't been to church for a while.

Jay and I see how the enemy is lying to individuals who are feeling rejected by God's love because they have not been following the rules within man's religious church system. They feel that you have to go to church *or else*! Sometimes we hear, "How could God possibly love me *again?*" God's love for His created ones is not based on the fact that the person decides to walk into a church building. I have been in plenty of church buildings that were love-less churches where there was such a superficial atmosphere of words without love that it was sucking the life right out of the people.

I remember several times when I was inside a church building, I could hear the "religious" thoughts that people around me were thinking as they looked at Jay and I. I have been to enough churches and heard enough church goers talk to know these religious thoughts. A few thoughts I hear are, "Oh good, another tither" or "Yes, more free help for us."

Too often as God's people gather together the spiritual atmosphere is filled with many words that seem to be genuine and caring. Mostly, those words are just a superficial greeting or an obligatory, "How are you?" or, "I'll pray for you." These words are too often spoken without love or intention of follow through. They are love-less. The words have become a part of their religious church system.

As I entered many of these church buildings the Holy Spirit would reveal His true wisdom to me. I would discern in the spirit that the thickest part of the atmosphere was gathered above and over the inside entrance doors where the church greeters stood. A church building's atmosphere can be full of dry dead bones with no life in most of its leaders and members.

Why do so many of the individuals we meet on the streets of Asheville believe that God's love is *only* available to them inside a church building? Why is it not available to them outside the church building? I believe these loveless spiritual words have extended far beyond the church building. I believe many believers in churches all over America are being strangled by a religious spirit, a blinding spirit, and a judgmental spirit to the point where they can't fully receive the love of God or fully give it out.

Inside and outside the church, people are being attacked by these spirits in their minds, hearts and souls. They are being suffocated. Let us all continue to battle in the spirit together as we ask Jesus to send out His army to pull down these strongholds, to expose them, and move them out for good! Then the atmosphere of dry dead bones will come back to life. They will breathe in His love and breathe out an atmosphere of love to others!

In 2014, Jay and I were asked by believers we love to visit an up and coming mega church that they had been attending. It was growing rapidly. As a family they really enjoyed all the church had to offer families with children and they were very curious as to our thoughts about their church. Jay and I love to worship with other believers and we were glad to attend.

When we walked into the church, I immediately saw

that it had all the bells and whistles and because the church was rapidly expanding, they organized outreach churches called campuses.

On this particular Sunday, their pastor was physically preaching at one of the other campuses. Suspended from the ceiling in our church building were several cutting-edge screens to view his sermon presentation. There are pros and cons to modern media technology.

We took our seats inside the meeting room. The worship team began to sing and play as they stood on a stage in the front of the room for all to see. They had a booming sound system.

The Holy Spirit was stifled because the worship team had to be finished worshiping at a precise time. All campuses had to synchronize the worship services since the pastor was going to be live streaming. It's very sad to me when a church claims to be spirit filled and led but puts the Holy Spirit on man's timeline.

The worship music was playing and in no time at all I was deep into worship. I entered into my chamber of worship and began to go in deeper but then God asked me to stop, open my eyes and look at the people in front of me, behind me, off to my left, and off to my right. As I looked, God opened my eyes into the spirit realm to show me what He saw.

I was not prepared for this but the people I looked at all around me, people I did not know, were standing stiff as could be and their eyes were life-less as if they were Zombies. Their bodies took on the appearance of sickened dry dead bones. It was the weirdest thing I've seen, and I have seen a lot of strange and mysterious things in the spirit.

I was shocked and a bit horrified, but I was calm and in control. God was bringing to my mind the event in scripture when the Spirit carried away Ezekiel, God's servant, and showed him this......*"The Lord took hold of me, and I was carried away by the Spirit of the Lord to a valley filled with bones. He led me around among the old, dry bones that covered the valley floor. They were scattered everywhere across the ground. Then He asked me, "Son of man, can these bones become living people again?" "O Sovereign Lord," I replied, "you alone know the answer to that." Then He said to me, "Speak to these bones and say, 'Dry bones, listen to the word of the Lord! This is what the Sovereign Lord says; Look! I am going to breathe into you and make you live again!"* Ezekiel 37:1-5.

About then, the worship ended and the people were asked to sit down, the pastor was about to begin his sermon. I remember writing down new revelations that my Father was speaking to me throughout the entire sermon. As I was writing and listening to the pastor's sermon, I realized his sermon was based on dry bones.

I believe God had also been showing and revealing to this pastor the valley of dry dead bones in his congregation. I bless this pastor for obeying Christ and not being afraid to speak a sermon of truth that was giving warning with positive yet righteous correction.

A few years later I went again to visit this same church and this time we sat down on white chairs in the back row in the middle section of the meeting room. As I looked off to my left and off to my right, I noticed there were many, many empty white chairs. I was told that the pastor would be preaching from another campus so I never did get the opportunity to personally meet and encourage this pastor.

Just before the worship team began to worship, I saw in the spirit, and felt it in the earthly realm, false angels come in through several entrance doors. They began to march in single file down each isle and one by one sat in every single empty white chair. It was very obvious to me that many of the people did not take heed to the dry dead bones warning and constructive words spoken to them to come back to life the previous time I had been there to visit. I felt sadness for each one as it was their own free will in refusing to wake up! Each one knew deep inside their man spirit, where the spirit of God dwells, that they were dry dead bones and they needed a new breath of life from Him in order to come alive again.

As worship began, I was again deep into my worship chamber when God asked me to stop and speak out loud and give this body of believers a message from Him. I said, "Yes." God shared with me that He would cause the instruments and the singers on stage to be silent. Then I should speak as loud as I could and not stop until the words I receive stop flowing.

A few seconds later God did what He said He would do. Everything became silent and I spoke loud and clear. I usually close my eyes and in the Spirit I see a scroll and words one by one will appear in a beautiful flowing script from an invisible feathered pen. The words are alive with movement on the scroll. All I do is read them. I use my voice to speak them out loud for all open ears to hear.

This time was different, instead of reading the words from the scroll, I was to keep my eyes slightly open while I spoke. The words came forth. I knew what to say. I spoke the words loud and clear. They were words from God telling them to wake up, to listen, and to come alive. The words were a lot like the words the pastor had spoken to them the last time I was there. I knew everyone was able to hear because it was so quiet you could hear a pin drop.

As I spoke the last few words, the musicians began to play, drowning out the last few words from God as if nothing had happened. I obeyed God and finished. It was so strange. I have never experienced anything like this before and the only word to best describe what happened next was **unresponsive.**

I asked God to fill me in on this unresponsiveness. He led me to turn my head around to the left and look at the few people standing in the row right behind me. He showed me their confirmation by their smiling faces. These few people were alive! They heard every word loud and clear, as did the believers I came to church with, but the others were unresponsive.

The Holy Spirit is leading me to share two scriptures *"And He said unto them, He that hath ears to hear, let him hear."* Mark 4:9 (KJB) and the other scripture is found in Revelation 2:7, *"Those who have ears should listen to what the Holy Spirit says to the churches. I will allow those who overcome to eat from the tree of life in God's paradise."*

As I continued to look around, I began to rejoice and be filled with joy because the false angels of light LEFT the building! God blew them OUT of their seats and OUT the door! Talk about the breath of God! I have a good hunch they were the ones who were causing all the interference spiritually by trying to close up the ears of the people so they would remain deaf and unresponsive.

When the service was over we left and as we were

talking in the car on the ride home, I learned that this pastor was being attacked by the leaders and various members in charge of ministries. It was becoming very obvious to me this pastor really did not have a voice in this body of believers, especially God's voice through him, and the sound of his voice kept falling on deaf ears.

I learned a great deal from the Lord through these two experiences. First, how to speak out with my God voice even if many do not want to listen. Second, there is always hope. I believe in miracles because you and I have the honor to battle in the spiritual realm for all those we see or meet who are deaf or dry dead bones and we will win the battle. They will hear and come back to life again.

We can be like Ezekiel by speaking out with our God voice, in the spirit, and command those dry dead bones in the valley to come alive again and breathe. You can't hear anything when you're dead! Let's remember the church is alive and living inside each and every one of us who are followers of Christ! Keep going up and into your own open chamber and you will always be open to use your gifts at a moment's notice!

It is good to meet with God's people often. It is good to not tolerate any evil spirits or any religious church system of man. The church is so much more than a building. Don't allow these spirits to take your breath away or dry you up to become dry dead bones. A church building is just that, a stone building. Never worship a building made by man. Never allow the building to become your tomb!

Seven

Freedom Chamber

When we choose to obey and move out in the freedom and the power of the Holy Spirit, the lost in Christ and even the found in Christ who are in slumber will be ignited to spiritually wake up. Even the physically dead will jump up and come back to life.

The last week of August 2013, our second son Josey, his wife Stephanie, and our two granddaughters, Destiny and Norah, came for a visit. On their last full day with us I was led by the Holy Spirit to run out to Walmart to purchase surprise gifts for them. I was supposed to put these gifts in their van before they left in the wee hours of the next morning.

I remember asking Jesus to lead me through the store to find each gift so I could return home quickly. Jesus always has his own timing when opportunities arise for Him to be glorified. I remember being at the back of the store when a loud, clear voice came over the store's intercom, "If there is a doctor, a nurse or EMT in the store please come to the front registers."

I asked Jesus if I should go up front and he said, "No, gather up your last gifts." So I did. And when I placed my last gift in my cart close to 20 minutes later, Jesus said, "Go to the front." He led me to the middle isle. When I reached the front of the store I was in perfect alignment for my next assignment.

There was confusion there as a man was lying on the floor apparently experiencing some sort of heart failure and he was not breathing. The man's skin looked like wax and it was a greyish color as if he had been prepared for burial. The police or ambulance had not yet arrived. A woman was holding the man's head in her lap as he lay on his back on the floor. Two employees kept onlookers at a distance.

I left my cart and walked to the commotion. Jesus allowed me to get within a few steps of the man lying on the floor. The manager and the few employees patrolling the area looked right through me, never asking me to leave yet pushing other people back who stood next to me and around me.

I remember the look of terror on the face of the woman who was standing a few steps to my left who I discerned to be his wife. She looked at me and then back down to her loved one lying on the floor. I was extremely calm and confident as I asked Jesus, "Do you want me to pray the spirit of death out of this man and the spirit of life back in?" Immediately Dad said, "Yes." So I prayed!

I gave the order for the spirit of death to leave. I spoke only loud enough for the man's wife, who was still standing only a few steps to my left, to hear me. It was so much fun because as soon as I commanded with the authority in Jesus' name for the spirit of life to return to this man, he jumped up to his feet in one fluid movement.

I knew in the spirit there were two angels, one standing to his left and one standing to his right. They both bent down placing their hands under each of his arms and in perfect unity set him up with effortless ease. I started to laugh with joy as these two invisible angels were having fun lifting him up and standing him on his feet.

The man, now full of life, looked a bit stunned as he started to bolt for the exit door saying, "I have to go home now." The employees around him protested and physically had to hold him back as he kept trying to leave. It took a while, but the man finally gave up and sat down until the ambulance showed up. His wife found out that day how real Jesus is. It was His name she heard spoken seconds before her husband woke up from death with renewed life entering into his body. I would have loved to have gone home with them to listen in on their conversation about what had happened. The spoken name of Jesus is life!

When my assigned opportunity was complete, I was released to go. I gathered up my cart like the rest of the shoppers and headed to an open register and proceeded to check out.

I was pleasantly surprised to see the elderly check out woman was someone who experienced the healing touch of Jesus through my obedience a few months prior when I was shopping at this store with my daughter, Tanique. Let me share with you our experience at that time.

I remember pushing our cart to the last check out register available. Tanique and I began to place our purchases on the belt runner. The elderly checkout woman quickly took out a prescription bottle from the pocket of her work smock and was contemplating whether to quickly take a pill before proceeding to check us out. I noticed she decided to wait and then set the bottle on her register while apologizing to us for her delay.

The expression on her face revealed that she was in severe pain. She began to massage the top part of her right shoulder and seemed to be having difficulty grabbing and scanning our purchases and placing them in bags.

While we looked on and tried our best to help her, Tanique and I both felt love and compassion for her. Next thing I knew God began to give me direction, telling me to take hold of the woman's right hand as she began to give me my change back. As she did, I was directed to speak a simple prayer out loud asking Jesus to take away her severe shoulder pain. Tanique was quickly alerted by Jesus to join in by quietly praying in her spiritual heavenly language. Ephesians 6:18 *"And pray in the Spirit on all occasions with all kinds of prayers and requests. With this in mind, be alert and always keep on praying for all the Lord's people."*

While Tanique prayed, she could begin to see in the spirit what I was experiencing. As I held this woman's hand, I felt the glory power of God's healing bubble up in my spirit. It began to rise up from my lower left abdomen area and flow straight up my left side over and into the top of my left shoulder. Then with great force, the power ran down from the top of my left shoulder continued down my left arm, straight through my fingertips and then surged into the fingertips of this woman's right hand. It surged through her hand, up her right arm, and directly into the area of severe pain at the top of her right shoulder.

The glory healing power knocked her back a step and she experienced complete healing and absolute freedom from the pain. This beautiful elderly woman believed and received. She knew exactly what Jesus had done because it was his name she heard as the power of his life flowed into her body to heal her wound. She thanked us over and over again and then we quickly left her praising God.

I turned back to look and saw her face all lit up with a glowing smile. She picked up the prescription bottle and put it back into her smock pocket. Free of pain, she continued to check out the next customer. I remember the minute we were out of her sight and standing at the exit doors to leave, I paused with Tanique and continued to battle the enemy that he would not interfere with her healing. When I knew I had complete victory, we left and continued on to do some more shopping!

I love going out and getting into some really "Good God Trouble" either alone or with others. But I have more to tell you about what happened after the man had collapsed in Walmart and then was restored to life again.

As I mentioned, after the man jumped up, I pushed my cart over to check out my purchases. As I approached the checkout lane, I immediately recognized the elderly woman checking me out as the woman whose shoulder Jesus had healed on that earlier visit. I was so pleased that she did not recognize me. This is the way I like it after God flows through me. I want to be quickly forgotten and Jesus quickly remembered for what His love has done. I love being his free agent to bring His freedom, His love, and His power to set all the captives FREE!!!

Well, as I placed my items on the belt, she greeted me and then began to tell me that she had a similar experience to what had just happened to the man who collapsed. She began to share with me that one week prior she had finished taking her break in the break room at the back of the store. She had taken a few steps out the door of the break room and stopped because she felt very dizzy. The next thing she knew she was headed up to the pearly gates and she knew without a doubt that her spirit was on its way up to Heaven. She was overwhelmed with great joy and anticipation but then she was suddenly pulled back into her body and immediately opened her eyes to see a few employees crouched down by her side.

I loved listening to her because she was so at peace and so calm as she explained this experience to me. She continued to share with me her life in Christ. She was concerned for her daughter who still needed to accept Jesus in her heart and be filled with His baptizing power from heaven.

I felt led to simply pray in authority a short prayer. I said, "Jesus make yourself real to her daughter." I was discerning that this woman still has assignments to finish and the first one is her daughter. I believe after many of her assignments are complete then her race will be won and she will cross the finish line into Victory! I do not even know the name of this woman but one thing I do know, I will spend eternity with her and her daughter and each of us will be given a new name as it says in Revelation 2:17 *"And I will give to each one a white stone, and on the stone will be engraved a new name that no one knows except the one who receives it."*

"On His robe and on His thigh He has this name written: **"KING OF KINGS AND LORD OF LORDS."** Revelation 19:16

From my chamber window, I will often see the citizens of Heaven and various activities going on in heaven. One time, I saw colorful markings on a female and I remember the entire side of her face had markings, like a tattoo. The markings resembled a long flowing, wavy thin string of the most beautiful and delicate tiny flowers. I can not even begin to describe how each flower was blooming with its own unique color. Each color seemed to have been marked with light. God is light so it makes perfect sense to me that His light creates incredible beauty. It was stunning!

Eight

Spirit Chamber

1 Corinthians 2:13,15 *"When we tell you this, we do not use words of human wisdom. We speak words given to us by the Spirit, using the Spirit's words to explain spiritual truths. "We who have the spirit understand these things, but others can't understand us at all."*

I love to go up and in to meet with Jesus in my special *Spirit* chamber. I can quickly go up and enter in anytime. It is a place where I continue to be taught deeper spiritual insights. I am taught when I should speak and when I should not speak.

Matthew 7:21 *"Not all people who sound religious are really godly. They may refer to me as 'Lord,' but they still won't enter the Kingdom of Heaven. The decisive issue is whether they obey my Father in Heaven."*

Religious Spirit

Have you ever had the Holy Spirit lead you into a spiritual but non-threatening conversation with someone who professes to be a Christian only to have that person look at you like you were speaking another language from another planet? I have, but then when I would talk to the same person about non-spiritual things the person will readily jump into the conversation.

1 Corinthians 2:14 explains to us why people sometimes do not understand. *"But people who aren't Christians can't understand these truths from God's Spirit. It all sounds foolish to them because only those who have the Spirit can understand what the Spirit means."* I have experienced this scripture come to life frequently and I expect it will continue to happen.

It doesn't take long into a conversation with someone for me to quickly discern that a religious spirit is rising up in the person's soul. I can easily discern this spirit and hear it speak through the person's mouth using words to argue or words to debate with me. I do not argue back. I do not debate with this religious spirit. Instead, I battle in the spirit on a spiritual level. I will only whisper under my breath a command to the religious spirit to be silent and not interfere while I am speaking with the person.

A whispered command in Jesus' name contains

the blood authority given to me, and to you, by the Father. As it is spoken, it is heard loud and clear in all the heavens, on all the earth and under the earth. The religious spirit must obey the Holy Spirit of God. In fact, it must bow to the name of Jesus as it is declared in Philippians 2:10 *"So that at the name of Jesus every knee will bow, in heaven and on earth and under the earth."*

I love to silence the religious spirit so the person will be able to listen to the Holy Spirit speaking through me. Because of that, the Holy Spirit is able to be heard inside the person's most inner being. It is He, and not I, who will stir and shake up their thinking. It is the Holy Spirit who will spark their curiosity and it is He who will speak pure words of love to gently draw the person closer into the Father's Heart. He does this so that one day this person too will understand spiritual truths. I love to watch this take place as the Holy spirit and I are in conversation with a person who claims to know God but actually only knows *of* God.

One example of this is an experience I had in the summer of 2014 with a young twenty year old woman. I had seen her several times before at the swimming pool in the mountain community where we were living. It was a beautiful sunny warm morning. She and I had the pool all to ourselves. We both decided to sit on the wide circular steps which led down into the pool and lounge with half of our bodies in the water. I was keeping to myself because I did not want to interrupt her sunbathing. I was laying back with my elbows on the steps looking up at the sky and observing several angels and created beings in the clouds looking down on me. This is something I love to do on a daily basis.

As I was intently watching the sky this young woman asked me what I was looking at and so I told her. She had an amazed look of wonder on her face and wanted to hear more about living in the supernatural. As we talked, the Holy spirit led me to say to her, "I always knew who God was, but I didn't *know* Him." She was quiet for awhile and then she looked at me and repeated what I had said. She then told me this statement deeply affected her and that until this moment she realized that she really didn't know God. She never had anyone say this to her before and she thanked me. This young woman knew of God but she really didn't know God. This powerful spiritual truth from the Holy Spirit spoke to her inner most being and broke her thinking in two. It completely changed her spiritual atmosphere and shifted her thinking.

I only saw this young woman a few times after that at the pool but she comes to my mind at times and I pray for her in the spirit. I know without a doubt God will always make himself known to her so she will know Him and He will draw her to go up and into her own chamber to be with her God! As with this young woman, the Lord desires the same thing for others who the Holy Spirit sends my way to not only know about Him but to personally know him, one on one, and to learn how to worship Him for who He is.

Whenever the Holy Spirit chooses to reveal these truths to a person through me, His open vessel, I will see the expression on the person's face change as if for the first time they realize there really is a God who is who He says He is. *"For who is God besides the Lord? And who is the Rock except our God? It is God who arms me with strength and makes my way perfect."* 2 Samuel 22:32-33 (NIV)

Here are a few questions for us to think about... Is He spirit? Is He truth? Who is the worshiper? And, how should the worshiper worship Him? I found the answers as the Holy Spirit directed me to read John 4:23-24 *"But the time is coming and is already here when true worshipers will worship the Father in spirit and in truth. The Father is looking for anyone who will worship Him that way. For God is Spirit, so those who worship Him must worship in spirit and in truth."*

The time is already here to be true worshipers and we will worship Him in Spirit and in Truth! I choose to worship the Father that way by worshiping Him with my highest praise, in high places while in the Spirit. I have found that my chamber in Heaven is a place consumed by God's spirit, a place that was created for me to go up and into. It's a place where I am completely free to worship my Father, my God, in spirit and in truth.

I am free to actually try it out. In other words, I am able to practice with Jesus who stands right beside me. He guides me as I learn from Jesus how to bring forth high praise within my spirit which then carries me right into the throne room. Hebrews 13:15 *"With Jesus' help let us continually offer our sacrifice of praise to God by proclaiming the glory of His name."*

Praise words, Praise songs, Praise instruments, Praise music, Praise dance breaks up the atmosphere. It prepares my spirit to move deep into silent, intimate worship. I believe true spiritual worship is obtained when I am standing before my God undone and bowing down in reverent silence as I dwell in the pure and holy presence of my majestic God. Praise and worship go hand in hand and both can be stepped into anytime and anywhere in this Spirit chamber of worship.

PRAISE THE LORD YOUR GOD

Psalm 47:1 *"Come, everyone, and clap your hands for joy! Shout to God with joyful praise!"*

Psalm 150:4 *"Praise Him with the tambourine and dancing, praise Him with stringed instruments and flutes!"*

Psalm 9:11 *"Sing praises to the Lord who reigns in Jerusalem. Tell the world about His unforgettable deeds."*

Ephesians 5:19-20 *"Then you will sing psalms and hymns and spiritual songs among yourselves, making music to the Lord in your hearts. And you will always give thanks for everything to God the Father in the name of our Lord Jesus Christ."*

Psalm 98:4 *"Shout to the Lord, all the earth; break out in praise and sing for joy!"*

Psalm 134:2 *"Lift your hands in holiness and bless the Lord."*

SILENT WORSHIP IS MEDICINE FOR YOUR SOUL

Zechariah 2:13 (NIV) *"Be silent, O all flesh, before the Lord: for He is raised up out of His holy habitation."*

Psalm 95:6-7 *"Come, let us worship and bow down. Let us kneel before the Lord our maker for He is our God. We are the people He watches over, the sheep under His care. Oh, that you would listen to His voice today!"*

Exodus 34:8 (ESV) *"And Moses quickly bowed his head toward the earth and worshiped."*

Hebrews 12:28-29 (ESV) *"Therefore let us be grateful for receiving a kingdom that cannot be shaken, and thus let us offer to God acceptable worship, with reverence and awe."*

Psalm 132:7 (ESV) *"Let us go to His dwelling place; let us worship at His footstool."*

Habakkuk 2:20 (ESV) *"The Lord is in His holy temple; let all the earth be silent before Him."*

Psalm 29:2 (ESV) *"Ascribe to the Lord the glory due His name; worship the Lord in the splendor of holiness."*

1 Peter 1:16 (ESV) *"You shall be holy, for I am holy."*

When I do this, **ALL** of heaven breaks loose and not only can I hear myself singing high praises but I also hear the citizens, angels and created heavenly beings who are in the throne room singing eternal high praises to God. Their high praises will rise up and mingle together in with my high praises and soar up to the highest heights of heaven. It is a beautiful sound... and then I dance. *"The highest heavens and the earth and everything in it all belong to the Lord your God."* Deuteronomy 10:14

My veil opens up wide from my high praise for the veil has already been torn. Mark 15:37-38 *"Then Jesus uttered another loud cry and breathed His last. And the curtain (veil) in the Temple was torn in two, from top to bottom."* This scripture tells us the veil was torn in two the day Jesus died on the cross, giving us a free opening to walk through with Jesus right up and into the Fathers presence, right there in the throne room in Heaven.

I believe it is important that our veils stay open. I believe we are the only ones who can start to close our open veils. When we allow our veils to close, it's as if we are trying to stitch the two torn pieces back together again, to keep us safe inside our spirits; to protect us from all the difficult or cruel circumstances that surround us or seep into our lives.

Many have become worn out, angry, or bitter to the point they cannot praise and worship their Lord. If our veils are starting to be stitched back together, we can offer up our high praises and our own high praises will begin to pull out each stitch, one by one, until our veils are fully separated again and opened to have access to enter in. I really do not fully understand how this all works, I just know it does!

I encourage you to go up and into your own spirit chamber to worship God the Father. Jesus will help you. He is there to draw your spirit up and to walk with you through the open veil, bringing you right into the presence of the One True God who loves you. *"I am the Alpha and the Omega," says the Lord God, "who is, and who was, and who is to come, the Almighty."* Revelation 1:8 (NIV)

Heavenly Languages

1 Corinthians 14:14-15 *"For if I pray in tongues, my spirit is praying, but I don't understand what I am saying. Well then, what shall I do? I will do both, I will pray in*

the spirit, and I will pray in words I understand. I will sing in the spirit, and I will sing in words I understand."

I will never forget the first time I was taught by Jesus that I too could receive His gift and pray in unknown languages. I was 23 years old and had only been born again a short time when I received a spiritual baptism. This was not a baptism in water but a filling with the glory power of His Holy Spirit. Then the fire of His love gave to me a present, a heavenly language, the gift of tongues. Matthew 3:11 *"I baptize with water those who turn from their sins and turn to God. But someone is coming soon who is far greater than I am—so much greater that I am not even worthy to be His slave. He will baptize you with the Holy Spirit and with Fire."*

I remember like it was yesterday. It was in the evening and I was sitting alone under the covers on my bed talking to the lord before I went to sleep. I had my bible on my lap when I felt compelled to read Acts chapter 2. This chapter tells us what happened to all the believers who gathered together in a room to pray while waiting for the promised Holy spirit to come.

When I finished reading, I heard Jesus say to me, "This is for you too." I remember thinking, "OK." I really didn't know what to do but I felt a strong urge to simply speak out loud the Lord's prayer. It was the prayer of my childhood through my upbringing in the Lutheran church. So that is exactly what I did. I spoke out loud the Lord's prayer once and then I felt to speak it out again.

As I began to speak out the last sentence of the Lord's prayer, I remember a bubbling feeling, a bubbling of His love filling up inside of me and then flowing up my throat and out of my mouth. I heard myself speaking these very last words, "For thine is the kingdom and the power and the glory forever and ever amen," but these words were not in English they were in a language I did not know. Simple as that! I was speaking in a brand new tongue from Heaven. I soon realized I was shouting. The new words came from deep inside my spirit, from my lower left abdomen, and traveled up the inside of my body and out through my mouth. I continued to do this until the language stopped flowing.

I sat there a bit stunned and then I thought to myself, <u>God is so very real</u>! My faith in Him exploded into a blessed assurance that Jesus is truly mine. I then decided to try it again. I heard the words coming out in the same sounding language as before but as the words were increasing, I could hear a different sounding dialect. I could hear myself speaking this new language out from my mouth but in my mind, I could understand what was being said in English at the same time.

I quickly learned that I could sing in my new language to all the worship songs during a church meeting while those around me were singing the songs in English. I could even hear a new worship song in English and sing along with the new song in my new spiritual language. I would make up my own praise song and sing it in my new language while in my mind I knew what the words were in English. It was awesome and it still continues to be a natural part of my life today.

I love using my own personal prayer language anytime I want to. When I gather and meet with the body of Christ, I will use the gift of tongues and the gift of interpretation. I can give the message myself and then translate what I have said in English or when another person gives a message in tongues, if no one speaks out to translate, I will translate if that is what the spirit has decided for me to do.

I remember back in the mid 1990's a woman from the church congregation my family and I regularly worshiped with came up to me after a church meeting and asked me if I knew what I was saying when I prayed in my private heavenly tongues. I told her, "Yes, I do." She then asked me, "How do you do this?" I told her to ask Jesus to give her the interpretation in English so she could then hear it in her mind or speak the translation out of her mouth. I'll never forget the next time we were together at church she came running up to me all excited because she asked Jesus to help her and He did! I was so blessed she asked Him. She received because she believed.

Our Lord has placed so many gifts inside of you that are ready and waiting to explode up and out from you! It's so simple to go up and into the spirit chamber to be with Jesus. Simply ask Him to fill you with the power of His Holy Spirit and with His Fire of Love. Simply believe it, receive it, and let it flow!

Acts 1:5 (KJB) *"For John truly baptized with water; but ye shall be baptized with the Holy Ghost not many days hence."* In my first book, "Heaven's Chambers," in chapter 4 - Battle Chamber – I write about an experience where a battle was won by speaking out loud in heavenly languages and how these tongues defeated the kingdom of darkness. This battle is an example of how God will give us all the armor we need to defeat any enemy that threatens us. There are many new languages we can receive from the Holy Spirit for the different purposes and assignments we are sent to go on.

Here is an example of how God quietly yet powerfully broke up the camp of the enemy one afternoon. On a day in 2012, Tanique and I were sitting at a bistro table outside a cafe on the beautiful main street of Hendersonville, North Carolina. It was a warm, sunny summer afternoon. We noticed the dark activity of three young adults near us, two male and one female. They were sitting in the sunshine a few yards from our table. One of the men was most definitely from out of state. He was here with his two companions to make sure his packages were delivered to the right person. It was easy to assume the packages were drugs.

A dark heavy presence surrounded the three of them and they had somber eyes with cold, evil looks on their faces. The Lord led Tanique and I into a new experience which I believe will be happening a lot more among the brides of Christ as His Kingdom advances. Tanique and I started to talk back and forth to each other in our heavenly languages instead of English. We carried on in conversation and we both knew exactly what each other were saying. It was so funny because we were talking about how beautiful the day was and how we were enjoying our time together.

We felt the spiritual atmosphere change and then laughter and joy began to emerge. This heavenly atmosphere began to break up the atmosphere of darkness sitting a few yards away from us. The darkness was actually lifting off the faces of these three young people and before we knew it the three of them were joking around and laughing among themselves. It was amazing to witness the power that the language from heaven, spoken on the earth, did to shift and change the atmosphere from darkness to laughter and joy. We even noticed a father and his young son move closer to our table trying to figure out what language we were speaking, but all the while they too were full of smiles and laughter.

Psalm 126:2 (KJB) *"Then was our mouth filled with laughter, and our tongue with singing: then said they among the heathens, the Lord hath done great things for them."* You too can learn from the Father how to shift and change the dark atmosphere around you as you go out every day to live a powerful life in Christ. Have you tried out any new words lately? Mark 16:17 teaches each of us that we can! *"And these signs shall follow them that believe; In my name shall they cast out devils; they shall speak with new tongues."*

In first Corinthians chapters 12, 13 and 14 Paul explains to us a deeper teaching regarding this wonderful language that believers can receive. I encourage you to ask Jesus to guide you and teach you, and then try it out. You have nothing to lose! The Lord is waiting for His children to open up and allow His power to flow through them at any given moment.

There is another situation that had to do with speaking a new language, but this opportunity was a lot different than the one I just shared with you. I was taking a walk around our community in the fall of 2013. There was a landscaping crew of two men who were raking leaves on one property. As I walked past them, I heard both of them talking to each other in Spanish, which is a language I do not understand outside of a few phrases I remember from my Spanish class in high school.

As I began to walk near the men, I knew that they were talking about me even though I could not understand what they were saying. I was sure something was up and I knew that they knew I did not understand them. Jesus read my thoughts and knew that I wanted to know what they were saying to each other. I could hear their playful chuckling at me and my little Chihuahua, Lola. It was a time I would have liked to have had a good family friend walking with me who does speak Spanish.

I really wanted Jesus to give me their language so I could talk with them. Instead, Jesus asked me to stop when I reached them and simply say hi and thank them for all of their hard work in the community. He also said to say, my Chihuahua is a little rat because she barked at them even before we reached them.

After I said this, a look of shock was on their faces and they both seemed embarrassed. I continued to talk to them for a little while and then continued on with my walk. Jesus told me they were laughing because they had said to each other in Spanish that Lola was a little rat. They figured I didn't have a clue what they were saying. They were not trying to be mean they were just having fun while working. Their work is tedious, it's hard and most people would not like their jobs.

I could sense they both had good hearts. Jesus wanted to teach them not to readily assume others could not understand them. I started laughing. Jesus joined in and He laughed harder than I did.

Nine

Love Chamber

His Love Is Amazing

1 John 4:16-21

"God is Love, and all who live in love live in God, and God lives in them.

And as we live in God, our love grows more perfect. So we will not Be afraid on the day of judgment, but we can face Him with confidence because we are like Christ here in this world.

Such love has no fear because perfect love expels all fear. If we are Afraid, it is for fear of judgment, and this shows that His love has Not been perfected in us.

We love each other as a result of His loving us first.

If someone says, 'I Love God,' but hates a Christian brother or Sister, that person is a liar; for if we don't love people we can see, how can we love God, whom we have not seen?

And God himself has commanded that we must love not only Him But our Christian brothers and sisters, too."

So then... are we to only love our Christian brothers and sisters? Is it OK to hate and not love those who are not Christians?

Does God hate? Or Does God only Love?

The Holy Spirit led me to read two scriptures as He answered my two questions. The answer to the first question is found in Proverbs 6:16-19 (ESV) *"There are six things that the Lord hates, seven that are an abomination to Him: haughty eyes, a lying tongue, and hands that shed innocent blood, a heart that devises wicked plans, feet that make haste to run to evil, a false witness who breathes out lies, and one who sows discord among brothers."* The answer to the second *love* question is found in Matthew 5:43-45 (ESV) *"You have heard that it was said, 'You shall love your neighbor and hate your enemy.' But I say to you, love your enemies and pray for those who persecute you, so that you may be sons of your Father who is in heaven. For He makes His sun rise on the evil and on the good, and sends rain on the just and on the unjust."*

I believe we are to love all the people God has created past, present, and future. We can hate the evil acts of sin, *"For all have sinned and fall short of the glory of*

God." Romans 3:23 (ESV), but We Must Forgive! We must love! We must allow God's everlasting love to flow through us, His open vessels. Brides of Christ we can choose to stand up in the Spirit and daily decree warfare prayers for all the lost souls around us to be forever set free. We must snatch them all from the evil one so they too will rise up in Christ. Heaven's highest love will fill our hearts while we live and move on the earth and it will grow to the point where we will operate only in His agape Love. This kind of love will expose and destroy every enemy of darkness!!! **God's Kingdom Age** has arrived. "*He has delivered us from the domain of darkness and transferred us to the kingdom of His beloved Son.*" Colossians 1:13 (ESV)

Gift of Love

"*God gave us His gift of love, His son sent to us from heaven to earth in human form so we could love as He loves.*" After the Holy Spirit wrote this statement through me, He led me to find this poem by Helen Stiner Rice, (On Wings of Love) It says it all...

The priceless gift of life is love

For with the help of God above

Love can change the human race

And make this world a better place

For love dissolves all hate and fear

And makes our vision bright and clear

So we can see and rise above

Our pettiness on wings of love

We must love in order to get along with each other and we must let go of our pettiness. God helps us to love the unlovable by flowing His love through us. His love will dissolve all hate and all fear. It's His fire of love that will burn up hate, burn up fear, dissolve and extinguish them.

I remember on May 12, 2016, I was up and in the chamber and I was asking God "Why do I have no fear?" I do not have fear. Even when I battle darkness I do not have fear. He led me to read His Holy Scriptures to answer my question. The scripture was 1 John chapter 4 and the verses were 16-21 *"We know how much God loves us, and we have put our trust in him. God is love, and all who live in love live in God, our love grows more perfect. So we will not be afraid on the day of judgment, but we can face him with confidence because we are like Christ here in this world. Such love has no fear because perfect love expels all fear. If we are afraid, it is for fear of judgment and this shows that His love has not been perfected in us. We love each other as a result of His loving us first. If someone says, "I love God," but hates a Christian brother or sister, that person is a liar; for if we don't love people we can see, how can we love God, whom we have not seen? And God himself has commanded that we must love not only him but our*

Christian brothers and sisters, too."

God on His throne answered me with the exact same scripture verses I had written in the beginning of this Love chapter. He led me to write them down again. If we will only love, all hate and all fear inside our hearts will not be found. Matthew 22:37-40 *"Jesus replied," 'You must love the Lord your God with all your heart, all your soul, and all your mind,' This is the first and greatest commandment. A second is equally important; 'Love your neighbor as yourself.' All the other commandments and all the demands of the prophets are based on these two commandments."*

In Luke chapter 10 verses 25-37 we read that an expert in religious law stood up to ask Jesus a few questions. One question was "Who is my neighbor?" Jesus replied by using the illustration of The Good Samaritan. This story is telling us our neighbor can be someone we do not even know. This is a different thought than what we usually think. Mostly we think of our neighbors to be only those who live in our community, our neighborhood. But Jesus is telling us that everyone He created is considered to be our neighbor.

I don't know about you, but I need God's love to flow through me continually so I can love as He loves. I need to love NOT with a fourth or a third or even with half of my heart but with my whole heart, with ALL of my heart!

There are many people we come in contact with every day who are evil, who hate, and even when you love on them in Christ, they often will not love you back.

Love is a choice and love must have actions. Love is not based entirely on a tingling feeling of love, whether it be a romantic love or a friendship love. I have met people, couples, who say they have a love-hate relationship, but I don't think that is good at all. We do have times when we don't agree with another person or they hurt us physically, verbally or emotionally but it is possible to love them in God's love even when they have come against us and caused great hurt to our hearts. We must be willing to forgive. We must forgive all transgressions from those who have come against us no matter the degree. And, we must ask God to help us to forgive even when we feel we can't.

If we speak, "I choose to forgive _____," then by saying their name and the transgression, God will begin the process of healing the hurt inside our hearts. His love will then flow through us and out to them. It doesn't mean we have to stay near to them and allow the cycle of abuse to continue, or to expect them to receive our forgiveness, or even give their forgiveness back to us, but through God's gift of love we must love.

God loves us. He is our true Dad. I believe God knows how to help each one of us to forgive. He is the only one who truly knows our personalities and what we need when we need it. He is a supernatural God and He will help us to even forgive Him.

We view forgiveness as something we do for the transgressor. Something that we need to do because of something someone has done to us, the emphasis being on the transgression, the offense. Forgiveness is about the hurt we are feeling, the resentment we took upon ourselves. So, when I talk about forgiving God, what I want to keep in mind is that forgiveness is letting go of the hurt and resentment, even toward God. Not that He has done anything wrong but that we've harbored hurt and resentment toward Him.

Whenever I feel transgressions come against me and hurt rise up, I run up and into His chamber of love where Jesus has a way of making it all right. God is never wrong. He knows how to console and counsel me and give me great advice because not only does He love me with an everlasting Love, but He also loves the transgressor. *"Forgive us our trespasses as we forgive those who trespass against us and deliver us from evil."* I love all the words Jesus taught us in the Lord's Prayer. I pray it a lot and its words are powerful inside of me. If you have never learned them then I encourage you to pray these words often. Here they are;

"Our Father who art in Heaven

Hallowed be thy name,

Thy kingdom come,

Thy will be done

on earth as it is in Heaven.

Give us this day our daily bread

and forgive us our trespasses

as we forgive those who trespass against us.

Lead us not into temptation

but deliver us from evil.

For thine is the kingdom and the power

and the glory forever and ever. Amen."

This is one of several prayers I learned when I was a child growing up in the Lutheran church. I would say this prayer often because it was the only way I knew how to talk to God at that time. I remember feeling the power of the words and I knew there must be something more to God than just this prayer.

When I was 23 years old, I cried out to God to make himself real to me and I experienced this prayer's power. God's kingdom came in and invaded my heart. His fire of Love and the power of heaven exploded inside of me. Heaven and earth became one in my life at that moment and His glory has never left me but continues to grow within me.

"And I pray that Christ will be more and more at home

in your hearts as you trust in Him. May your roots go down deep into the soil of God's marvelous love. And may you have the power to understand, as all God's people should, how wide, how long, how high and how deep his love really is. May you experience the love of Christ, though it is so great you will never fully understand it, Then you will be filled with the fullness of life and power that comes from God." Ephesians 3:17-19. God fills us with His love so we can love Him, ourselves, and all people. God gives to us His love and without His love we can't love God or pour out His love to others.

"Love is not only something you feel; it is something you do."

(David Wilkerson, founder of Teen Challenge.)

Ten

Command Chamber

COMMANDMENTS GOD GAVE TO MOSES...

1. *"I am the Lord your God, who brought you out of the land of Egypt, out of the house of bondage. You shall have no other gods before Me.*

2. *"You shall not make for yourself a carved image, or any likeness of anything that is in heaven above, or that is in the earth beneath, or that is in the water under the earth; you shall not bow down to them nor serve them. For I, the Lord your God, am a jealous God, visiting the iniquity of the fathers on the children to the third and fourth generations of those who hate Me, but showing mercy to thousands, to those who love Me and keep My commandments.*

3. *"You shall not take the name of the Lord your God in vain, for the Lord will not hold him guiltless who takes His name in vain.*

4. *"Remember the Sabbath day, to keep it holy, six days you shall labor and do all your work, but the seventh day is the Sabbath of the Lord your God. In it you shall do no work: you, nor your son, nor your daughter, nor your male servant, nor your female servant, nor your cattle, nor your stranger who is within your gates. For in six days the Lord made the heavens and the earth, the sea, and all that is in them, and rested the seventh day. Therefore, the Lord blessed the Sabbath day and hallowed it.*

5. *"Honor your father and your mother, that your days may be long upon the land which the Lord your God is giving you.*

6. *"You shall not murder.*

7. *"You shall not commit adultery.*

8. *"You shall not steal.*

9. *"You shall not bear false witness against your neighbor.*

10. *"You shall not covet your neighbor's house; you shall not covet your neighbor's*

wife, nor his male servant, nor his female servant nor his ox, nor his donkey, nor anything that is your neighbor's.

Matthew 22:36-40 *"Teacher, which is the most important commandment in the law of Moses?" Jesus replied, 'You must Love the Lord your God with all your heart, all your soul, and all your mind.' This is the first and greatest commandment. A second is equally important; 'Love your neighbor as yourself.' All the other commandments and all the demands of the prophets are based on these two commandments."*

The Ten Commandments are based on these two commands to love. Why did God give us His Ten Commandments? I believe for the same reason we give our own children rules to follow in our homes. We love them and we have a great desire to protect them by making sure they know what is right and what is wrong. We invest our lives into our sons and our daughters. Even more so, God invests Himself, the Trinity, into us His sons and His daughters. It is these LOVE Commandments from God's heart that we need to obey. We need to teach our own children to respect and obey these commandments as well as to their children so this cycle of obedience for God's Holy Commandments will continue on into our future generations. We must raise up and care for our own children in the same way God lovingly cares for and raises us up to become mighty men and women of God. Our lives should abide within the rules of these commandments and His love should pour out through us to our own children.

His love is not abusive. His love does not belittle. However, His love will correct our wrong and His love will bring discipline to protect us like we discipline our own children. His love is a love so strong that He sent His only son to pour out His life blood and die for you and I. His love made the way for our hearts to be able to repent and accept His forgiveness even in our times of ignorance, even in our times of rebellion or selfishness, even when we fall short and completely mess it up by breaking one of His commandments.

I want you to remember that even in our weakness we must not run away and hide from God. We must run to God during those times, remembering His love will always make a way for us to admit our sin and ask His forgiveness, to renounce and turn away from our sin so we can go back up and into His heart of love.

God's love is a fire, a fire that will burn inside His children's hearts and spread out of control until it consumes our entire being. I think of my forgiven sins as being thrown into the beating Heart of God where they land on His stones of fire. I watch as His fire burns up and consumes all of my sins until they disappear, evaporate, and are gone forever. And remember how far they will travel. *"As far as the east is from the west, so far has He removed our transgressions from us."* Psalm 103:12 (NIV)

"And the Lord spoke to you from the fire. You heard His words but didn't see His form; there was only a voice. He proclaimed His covenant, which He commanded you to keep----the Ten Commandments----and wrote them on two stone tablets." Deuteronomy 4:12-13

The Holy Spirit will help us to be successful in following God's commandments to love. He will help us flee from any temptation and when He warns us to run, then Run! Sin is satan. Sin destroys you and those around you. When sin is committed in thought, word or deed it creates an opening and a evil spirit/demon can freely enter inside a heart, soul, mind and body. And, if the sin continues it will make an even larger opening for even more evil spirits to enter in and set up housekeeping.

This is not to say that each time a person commits a sin an evil spirit/demon will enter but when the sin continues it most likely will. Sin needs to be dealt with. To deal with sin we need to see that it is sin, confess it to God, ask for forgiveness, renounce the sin, break the sin curse, send out the demon of sin and stop doing the sin. Even sin against us through past generations can travel through our bloodlines to find a home inside you or I. It can even happen while we were growing inside of our mother's womb.

For example, if a baby was not wanted, a spirit of rejection and abandonment can enter into the fetus at any stage of development. I have experienced these two spirits which entered into me as a fetus. Jesus and I expelled them out to set me free. Curses will need to be broken and every evil spirit will need to be commanded to leave through the authority and blood power of Jesus. It's HIS power working through a believer to discern and expose all darkness that needs to be sent out from within a person's heart, soul, mind and body.

When evil spirits are gone from the area where they have taken up residence, the love of Jesus can be sent in to invade and fill the area that was once occupied with sin and darkness. His love will fill, heal, restore, and close the opening to the area that the evil occupied. God shuts the door and only through our own free will and sinful actions can the door to that area be opened again. Remember it only takes a peep hole for an evil spirit to start seeping in again through sin. His love kept inside us will maintain freedom in our heart, soul, mind and body. His love will keep the doors closed. Staying close to Jesus, praising, worshiping, reading His Holy word will help us to maintain our freedom.

At times, and like we often read in the bible, sending out evil spirits can be messy and it can be noisy. They would rather not go but it needs to be done and we can be trained by Jesus to help each other get free and stay free. Jesus and His disciples did this often and so can we. Every single person who lives on earth needs deliverance. Like it says in the Lords prayer, "...deliver us from evil." This also refers to evil being delivered out from where it has taken up residence inside the areas of our heart, soul, mind and body as well as in the atmosphere around us as we daily breathe and live in it.

When you and I became born again God's spirit made us brand new with His love! The spirit of God dwells inside our man spirit and will not be invaded with evil. But your heart, soul, mind and body are where the enemy loves to invade and set up housekeeping. Christians were born into sin just like those who haven't accepted God's forgiveness yet. We all were sinners before any of us accepted Christ. How many of us can keep ourselves completely free? If we never sinned in thought, word, or deed, then none of us would have a need for deliverance.

Our sins are forgiven at the cross but it says nowhere in scripture that the cross automatically evicted all the evil spirits out from the inside of a person who accepted Jesus as their Lord and Savior. If it were so, then how could we as born-again believers continue to fall into sin if evil spirits can't again gain entrance inside of us? Or, why then would we continue to struggle and never seem to get rid of sin we struggled with before and after our conversion?

Remember, satan is sin and he is the force behind sinful words, thoughts, or deeds. Scripture is full of people who struggled with sin before and after dedicating their lives to God. David, Saul and Solomon to name a few all gave their lives to God but yet all fell into sin. All of them needed deliverance. Jesus continues to teach me about the marine (water) spirits who have spellbound many in the church body since 300 AD. These are the ones who have believers believing that "Christians can't have demons." Praise God the spell has been broken but those who still believe this need to be unmasked from these false marine (water) spirits inside their mind, heart and soul because it is blinding them. God warns us in His second commandment to not make any carved image or any likeness or bow down to or serve that which is in the water or under the earth. These spirits need to come out!

A few of the job assignments satan sends his mind-blinding and very religious marine spirits on is to convince Christians and leaders to believe it is impossible to be infested with a demon after you are born again and made new. This spirit also convinces them to believe that sending demons out of a person absolutely doesn't happen today like it did when Jesus and His disciples walked on the earth. It even tries to say demons are harmless or don't really exist and the list of lies goes on and on.

We need to remember God declaring, "I am the same yesterday, today and forever" (see Hebrews 13:8.) God does not change! If you have any questions or concerns about this feel free to go up and into your own chamber and discuss these matters with the Father, Son and Holy Spirit. They love answering our questions and their truth will debunk all of satan's lies.

There is another revelation that I would like to share that I learned quite a while ago. Your soul cannot be sold to satan, to God or to anyone. It is impossible! Because of free will. God gave us free will to choose. You can choose to follow satan or God or another person, but your free will can never be compromised, it is not for sale. The enemy can't make us do anything nor can God. We can choose which spirit we want to fill us and it is that spirit which helps to motivate our choices.

We humans, and all of His created beings, have free will and it was lucifer who decided with his own free will to make a very bad mistake. He decided that he wanted to be God and rule heaven. Well, we all know how that turned out! Lucifer chose with his own free will, as did the angels who believed lucifer's lie, and rebelled against God.

God who sits upon His throne is omniscient. Our all-knowing God knew exactly what lucifer was thinking.

God knew all along about lucifer's prideful plan to claim himself as God and try to take over heaven. But God could not compromise lucifer's free will, so He allowed lucifer to work out his foolish plan. When lucifer and his followers made their move, it moved them right out of heaven. When a person "sells their soul to the devil" and even signs a contract in blood guess what; the blood of Jesus and your own free will to choose will cancel out this evil plan and will break that lie. But satan will tell you differently, he will say he owns you and no one can get you out of the contract you signed with him.

I remember listening to a famous singer who was being interviewed and I will never forget his response when asked what caused his great success all these years. He said, "I sold my soul to satan and now I have to hold up my end of the bargain." I wanted to tell this singer, "No, you don't!" I wanted to explain to this person that because God gave you free will your soul is not for sale! Even if you agreed to a blood contract and signed lucifer's "bill of sale." You can still be set Free!!!

It is so important to get the right information from God and not believe any lies from darkness. Before He died on the cross, Jesus taught his disciples, and us, in Luke chapter 11 how to pray through teaching us the Lords prayer. He taught us what to pray in this prayer with important words like, "Deliver us from evil." Now why would Jesus teach us this prayer and tell us to pray it often if after his blood was shed for the atonement and the forgiveness of past, present and future sins if no more sin could live or be found inside us?

Jesus knew that after He ascended to the Father we all would need continued deliverance from sin. We would need continued deliverance from invasion of demonic spirits intruding through our blood lines and from sin openings that gain entrance to live in our hearts, souls, minds and bodies.

Jesus had a deliverance ministry when he walked on the earth. He taught His disciples how to deliver. He provided us with His wisdom and His plan so every person can begin their process of deliverance from demonic evil spirits. Jesus will help us to maintain our freedom. It is a gift we can accept from Him but we must take the first step by asking Him to lead us in this process. We are to carry on with all of His ministries including deliverance because it is important.

Jesus performed a whole lot of deliverances by casting out devils. He would speak inner healing to the person's heart, soul and mind to make them whole. Jesus healed bodies and performed countless miracles as we read all throughout His Holy Bible. Deliverance and healing, healing and deliverance, go hand in hand. What a double blessing to receive!

I am only sharing as much as the Lord allows. I would share much more detail if this were strictly a book on casting out evil spirits and how to deal with the evil one, aka lucifer, and his band of fallen angels. Jesus can train you and He can lead you. I really want to encourage you with the fact that it is possible to do all the works Jesus did and His greater works yourself. He tells us this in John 14:12-14. When you get a chance read these verses in your bible because they are remarkable!

We learn truth by asking. Jesus loves to teach us how to pull down strongholds, how to expose evil, how to cast out evil, and how to fill up and keep a heart, soul, mind and body filled and maintained. If sin seeps in, we do it *again* through self-deliverance or with another believer. Jesus continues to teach me that it is good to experience an initial deliverance with the help of an experienced believer, and that self-deliverance can also be a great tool to be used and applied in the life of a believer. It is a daily process to begin to purify and maintain freedom from demonic evil spirits while living on this earth. Deliverance with healing is a wonderful and needed gift from God.

I have never experienced a shortage of people who are bound and looking to start the process of kicking satan out and keeping him out. The age of a person has nothing to do with it. The youngest person Jesus flowed through me to begin freedom was a toddler. Remember the enemy doesn't care about age, the younger the better.

Jesus sent me on an assignment in the summer of 2018 to a Big Lot's store here in North Carolina. I went to the isle where the rugs were located when a woman and her husband came to look at rugs while I too was shopping for a new rug. The woman started a conversation with me telling me she was sick because she had cancer. I shared with her that Jesus has taught me that cancer is a demon and I would be honored to pray with her to ask Jesus to take the demon of cancer out so her healing could begin.

She was excited and willing to be set free. I asked her a few questions and then this woman, along with her husband and myself, broke generational curses and prayed for her freedom right there in the middle of the rug isle at the Big Lot's store. That demon of cancer **left** and her freedom and healing began.

The one thing that struck me most after we prayed for her freedom was what this couple told me. They said they both have been asking Jesus to send someone to pray for them to help her with this cancer. They told me how much they loved attending their bible believing church but no one in church ever asked if they could pray for her this way. That broke my heart! I am only sharing a very short version of this assignment but one thing I know is that my Jesus walks with me wherever I go. He is the one who can heal and deliver anyone anywhere just like He did when He walked the earth so many years ago.

I remember how awesome it was when I began my own *kicking out* process. I love maintaining my Freedom! I encourage you to talk with Jesus about freedom, He will lead you, He will train you, He will move through you in His power and authority. He will send others to you or you to them. We can learn how to pray for each other to receive total freedom. God loves for His children to be together to pray, to battle, to deliver, to heal, to testify, to read the word, and to help each other grow closer to Him and unify in love. We should operate in all the gifts and use all the resources He has given each one of us for His Glory and His power through Jesus Christ our Lord and Savior, our King.

This is the way we should be functioning every time we meet and gather inside or outside of any church building, ministry, cell group, bible study, etc. Be the Church of Jesus Christ, His congregation, His Brides of power and let's all go out in Christ every single day and do His **Greater Works.**

I want to close this chapter with one of the verses I encouraged you earlier to read. I love this verse! John 14:12 *"The truth is, anyone who believes in me will do the same works I have done, and even greater works, because I am going to be with the Father."*

Eleven

Saturate Chamber

"Saturate yourself with me for I am Love, I am Joy, I am Peace, I am Power, I am Fire, I Am All You Need... I Am All You Need." These are the words that flowed from my fingertips as I typed them on my laptop. Wisdom and Truth from the one who will saturate you and me from the inside out. Truth that the I Am will not quit. The I Am will not stop saturating you and me to be fully soaked inside with His Love, His Joy, His Peace, His Power and His Fire with a double portion.

How do I know it is a double portion? Because, the last sentence of the words written "I am all you need," is repeated by the I Am a second time. He said it "Again." He will doubly bless you and me with His double portion of His Love, His Joy, His Peace, His Power, and His Fire! *"And God said unto Moses, I AM That I AM."* Exodus 3:14 (ESV) He repeated to Moses, "I AM," not once but twice. He repeated it "Again!"

I choose for the "I Am" to saturate me and to be completely involved in all of my decision making. I find it goes quicker and smoother when I have the master designer's input. This has become second nature to me. I ask Him *first* what He thinks so He will keep leading me into countless and new experiences as I live my life in Him.

I share many other experiences that are not included in my Heaven's Chambers book series on my www.HeavensChambers.com website. My website is always a work in progress as Jesus is always bringing new ideas, people, and assignments into my life! My website will give you the opportunity to write to me on the website your important comments, experiences, prayer requests and revelations too.

I love to hear from my readers on a more personal level. I also like being saturated with not only my readers' love for Christ but with the love from all believers I meet who make up the body of Christ. The love of God in you shines out and into me and I can pour that love right back into you. It keeps us all saturated in the Love of the Father. It keeps us connected. It gives us strength to make it through the hard times, as well as the great times, as we live our lives together in the body of Christ because we are listening and obeying the head of our body.

Colossians 1:18 *"Christ is the head of the church,*

which is His body. He is the first of all who will rise from the dead, so he is first in everything" So my thought is.... since Christ is FIRST in everything, shouldn't we simply go to Him first with all of our everything?

Ephesians 1:22-23 *"And God has put all things under the authority of Christ, and He gave Him this authority for the benefit of the church. And the church is His body; it is filled by Christ, who fills everything everywhere with His presence"*

1 Corinthians 12:26-27 *"If one part suffers, all the parts suffer with it, and if one part is honored, all the parts are glad. Now all of you together are Christ's body, and each one of you is a separate and necessary part of it."*

Aromas

Chocolate chip cookies. My entire bedroom was saturated with the aroma of freshly baked chocolate chip cookies coming right out of the oven. I could picture them on cooling racks and the smell was so intense I wanted to eat one cookie, or two, ok maybe three. It was late one night in 2015, Jay was still working in his office in our home and I had not yet fallen asleep. I quickly ascended up into my chamber in heaven to find out where this aroma was coming from.

Jesus met me in my chamber and began to tell me that heaven got together and decided to bake tons of chocolate chip cookies for the wedding feast because He knows that many of His brides love to eat chocolate chip cookies. I agreed with Jesus that this was a great idea. After our talk I lay on my bed looking up at my ceiling until I gently fell asleep to this amazing smell. When I woke up the next morning, there was still a faint smell of Heaven's chocolate chip cookies. I look forward to eating a ton of them!

I love it when I smell aromas from heaven. Some aromas I smell are apples, oranges, lilac flowers and bubble gum. One at a time, and without prior notice, a scent will fill the entire room I'm in or at times a small area where I am sitting or standing. It does not matter whether I am inside or outside my home.

I remember back in 2005 when we had a small prayer meeting of believers gather in our home. As we were allowing the Holy Spirit to have complete control of our meeting Jay and my sister-in-law both said they were smelling a flower fragrance. This was the first time one of heaven's scents came down and mingled into our midst. Jay continues to smell heaven scents and I am so glad I can join him in this special experience as heaven and earth combine together as one in our lives. It's a breath of fresh air!

Jesus led me to find what these aromas listed represent, each of which I have experienced.

Apples-sweet breath of beloved

Bubble gum-childlike

Chocolate-sweet spirit

Cookies-heavenly manna

Oranges-sweet companionship and love of the Lord

Roses-sweetheart-Jesus

I like the meanings behind my aromas. In fact, as I am typing this right now, I smell oranges and it makes me smile that my sweet Lord is with me. I am so looking forward to experiencing many more aromas as you, Jesus, bring them into each of our lives from heaven. I love all of His *new* that He brings into my life as I continue to be saturated in His love. Take some time today to…. Smell the Roses!

Song of Solomon 2:1 *"I am the rose of Sharon, the lily of the valley"*

Jesus you are the lover of my soul

Twelve

Light Chamber

Jesus is indeed the light that will shine into any darkness as he showed me in early 2011. He is the light that will reveal every secret that is hidden. His light exposes truth and His light exposes lies. His light will never leave, it is eternal. *"Then Jesus asked them, 'would anyone light a lamp and then put it under a basket or under a bed to shut out the light? Of course not! A lamp is placed on a stand, where its light will shine."* Mark 4:21

Jesus is the light! Does He live in you? Do you allow Him to shine through you? Mark 4:22 *"Everything that is now hidden or secret will eventually be brought to light"* I believe that sin always finds itself out but I think it is better for sin to be found out while we're still alive on the earth than in death. Darkness attacks and darkness tries to overtake us but this is what scripture says in Psalm 112:4 *"When darkness overtakes the godly, light will come bursting in."* To do what? Expose and take out the darkness!

Jesus will often ask Jay and I to walk into dark places to be His light. We do not become the darkness, but we shine to break up the darkness. Everyone is affected by the light and it's fun to be His light. Jesus must do the directing and we must do the following by listening carefully to His instructions. With the help of the Holy Spirit and His Holy Angels the results are eternal.

It was in 2013, Jay and I were walking on the streets of Asheville with our daughter Tanique and son Jonas. It was a perfect warm summer day in the early evening at around 6:30 p.m. We were walking the streets to see what kind of *Good God Trouble* we would be sent into and Tanique and Jonas led the way. It was fun to allow them the opportunity to hone in on their Holy Spirit listening skills as He directed them on which venue we were to enter and where to sit.

It wasn't long until they both headed into a music venue. This venue did not have a very good reputation. Often in the wee hours of the morning the police would be called to come as young adults tended to get too much to drink and fights would break out. A few times the incidents would be reported on the local news. Jay and I were not surprised that God sent us into this business. We are often sent into even darker places to light them up. There is nothing like on the job training in releasing individuals from darkness. There are times we are sent into businesses to break up the spiritual darkness. I will tell you about a business breakup assignment after I finish sharing this one with you.

It was a tastefully decorated place. Not a dump but we both discerned it did have some spiritually dark critters running around which I won't get into right now. It had great food, nice bartenders and servers, and an ample area for the D.J. to perform and for dancing.

As Jay and I followed several steps behind our kids we noticed there was only one bartender. Jonas and Tanique were already in conversation with him but the bartender did stop to greet us as well. The venue was completely empty except for one handsome couple in their early to mid-twenties sitting at a bistro table and they were in deep conversation with each other. Our kids were led to walk past them and sit on the next bistro table. The bistro tables were placed a few feet from each other in order to seat and serve as many customers as the fire code permitted. We were close to this couple.

A friendly server quickly came over and as the server was taking our order Jesus was talking to me about Matthew chapter 11, about what leaders in the church would say about His lifestyle and people He chose to be with. It was with all those sinners. They said Jesus was a glutton, a drunkard, and He feasted more than He fasted.

As we were talking, all of us were being filled with God's precious love and concern for this young couple. We were sent into this dark venue for the light to come bursting into their darkness. We must remember dark places are all around us, even more so in our places of worship. Every day ask for great discernment and keep your spirit open to flow His light of love out from you and into those who are searching in silence and are desperate for internal freedom.

As the four of us were having fun in our conversation, we noticed the young couple taking interest in what we were talking about and seemed interested as we were sharing with each other about Jesus. Soon we were introducing ourselves to each other and they pulled up their chairs to join us.

As the evening progressed Jay was ministering one on one to the young man who really had an unhealthy view of a woman's role in a relationship while Tanique, Jonas, and I were talking with the young girl. She, like Tanique, was a cosmetologist. Both 21 and both had been involved in relationships where the man did not treat them very well.

Later in the evening, the young girl and I were talking and I started a deep conversation with her about having a born-again relationship with Christ and being filled with His Spirit, living in His power and authority. I saw her face light up with such astonishment. Tears of hope began to well up in her eyes as she began to tell me that earlier in the week she had cried out to God to please tell her who Jesus was and how to find Him because her life had become so miserable, so terribly unbearable and sad.

It took her only a few seconds and sitting right there on our stools in the middle of darkness she was ready to repent, accept the blood sacrifice of Jesus on the cross, His death, His descending into Hell, and His glorious resurrection. She received forgiveness because she believed it with all her heart! I had the honor to be with her as she asked Jesus and His love to enter into her heart. I was humbled to pray with her to receive Christ and then to pray over her declaring heaven to release anointing on her to be filled up with God's Holy Spirit and glory power. Heaven was rejoicing and having a Party!

After she was made brand new, Jesus reminded me that prior and throughout the evening I noticed she kept asking me or others to repeat ourselves because she could not hear what we had said. She told me that she could not hear very well and that she had an unusual hearing loss. Whenever she was someplace where there was any kind of background noise, she could not hear the person she was talking directly to.

I asked her if we should ask Jesus to heal that hearing problem and her response was "Yes!" I had her stand up with me and I saw Jonas, who was led by the Holy Spirit, stand with us and in the noise of it all I placed each of my hands over her ears and prayed while Jonas prayed silently. Jesus was touching her as she had a childlike faith. It was that childlike faith of believing and receiving that restored her life and hearing to be made brand new. He answered our prayers. She was a sinner who was lost in the noise of the world. She has been found and *now* can hear Jesus.

I choose to be like Jesus and like Jesus I don't mind if religious people say I am a friend of sinners just like it says in Matthew 11:18-19 *"For John the Baptist didn't drink wine and he often fasted, and you say, 'He's demon possessed.' And I, the Son of Man, feast and drink, and you say, 'He's a glutton and a drunkard, and a friend of the worst sort of sinners!' But wisdom is shown to be right by what results from it."* The result of our loving on sinners is that this young girl went from being a sinner to being saved and is now a child of the Most High God!!!

Psalm 116:9 *"And so I walk in the Lord's presence as I live here on earth!"*

On a beautiful day in 2014 Jay and I arrived at one of the large grocery stores in Hendersonville, North Carolina to purchase a few groceries on our way home from an outing. We had just finished our Saturday afternoon drive along a few of the mountain roads and on the Blue Ridge Parkway. The views of the mountains and waterfalls on the parkway are spectacular. If you ever want to google the Blue Ridge Parkway in the Blue Ridge Mountains of Western North Carolina you will get an idea of how beautiful the area is.

Jay and I had gathered up our few items and headed to the register to check out and pay for our purchases. As we finished, we turned to leave and we walked toward the large glass enter/exit doors. We had only walked a few yards when all of a sudden time slowed down. Both Jay and I looked at each other and knew something dark, something evil had walked through the entrance door and it was headed right toward us and to the register we had left.

We continued to walk slowly as a tall slender man walked past us dressed in a button up shirt, worn out jeans, old looking boots, with long black shoulder length hair, a long thin face, and eyes pure black with evil that we could barely see the whites of his eyes. The minute we both gazed into his eyes we were shown in the spirit exactly what he came in this store to do. He was there to steal and to kill and was headed to our register.

Jay and I felt the glory anointed power of God rise up and out from each one of us and blast into this man's darkness. As we locked our eyes into his eyes, the evil looking at us knew that we knew exactly what kind of evil this dark demon had convinced this man to engage in! It was right there, in that second, in the spirit Jay and I together from within our spirits released the anointing power of God's glory light through us and right into this evil. God's Hosts joined in this spiritual battle to pierce this evil with the sword of the spirit and foil this evil plan.

The evil enemy inside the soul of this man retreated back down, wounded and defeated. This retreat released the man to be himself again but it caused the man to became confused because he had lost the power that gave him the strength and anger to steal and kill. This all happened in the short time we walked pass him to the exit door.

Jay and I walked out the door and began to walk to our vehicle. We walked past a light tan van parked outside the door. It was parked in a designated short-term pick up, drop off, space and the driver of the van was as evil looking as the tall slender man we just passed. He was waiting for his partner in crime to come back out. He was the get away driver. Our vehicle was parked in a front row stall close to the entrance and close to their van.

When Jay and I reached our vehicle and as we both were getting into our vehicle, we saw the evil man from inside the store hurry out of the exit door and quickly jump into the front passenger seat in the van. The driver pulled out of the reserved parking space and drove slowly past the back of our vehicle with both of their eyes gazing intently at Jay and I. When it was clear, Jay then backed up our vehicle out of the parking stall to follow close behind their van. But as they were slowly driving in front of our vehicle their van literally disappeared into thin air.

Jay and I started to laugh because we knew what was happening. The evil these two lost souls had asked to live inside of them is more than likely rooted in some very evil black magik and unfortunately their teacher is satan, the evil one. The van disappearing reminded me of the day when a young man astral-projected into our home. I will write about that in the third book but the point is... Christ's power and authority has already defeated the evil one. It is His power, it is the blood of Jesus, His name and His authority that lives in and flows through Jay and I that was able to take out the enemy. It's the power that stopped these two demonized men and foiled their plans. I know the reason they wanted to quickly disappear was because they were the ones terrified not us!

Jay and I walk in the presence of the Lord while we live on this earth because we have allowed heaven and earth to be glued into our spirits, our hearts, our souls and our minds. And you can be glued too! We choose to spend time with Jesus in our light chambers for it is a place to bask in His light. It is a place to sit and be saturated with His presence and with His power. It's really not hard to do at all. It's only a matter of taking the time to be alone with the Father, Son and Holy Spirit, the three in one. It's making yourself available. Ephesians 5:11,13-14 *"Take no part in the worthless deeds of evil and darkness; instead, rebuke and expose them. But when the light shines on them, it becomes clear how evil these things are. And where your light shines, it will expose their evil deeds. This is why it is said,*

"Awake, O sleeper,

Rise up from the dead,

And Christ will give you light."

Thirteen

Encourage Chamber

I want to take the time to encourage you, my reader, to press in and **Never Give Up**! You can do it! You can ascend up and into the heavens to meet with Jesus in your own special chamber, built especially for you! Our Father is always creating. He is a master builder. No wonder Jesus was a carpenter and loved to build and work with His hands. He is like His Father in Heaven and like Joseph His second dad on earth who too was a master carpenter. John 1:1-3 *"In the beginning the Word already existed. He was with God, and He was God. He was in the beginning with God. He created everything there is. Nothing exists that He didn't make."* Do you know *who* the word is referring to in this verse? *Who,* already existed?

I feel led by God not to give you the answer but to give you the opportunity for you and God to figure it out together, in your chamber. He will reveal to you who "*who*" is. I love to break down words in a scripture verse and ask questions while in my chamber. I am always encouraged by Him to keep on pressing in until He reveals to me His new revelation. I never feel embarrassed or foolish, in fact I feel absolutely Great! I feel absolutely encouraged!

Words from the Lord

My sweet, sweet children how I love you, how I adore you, how I want to gather you close to my heart and tuck you back inside of me to keep you safe. But instead I chose to live inside of you, to guide you from the inside and to give you life everlasting. I have made a way through my son to bring you safely back home to me and back into my heart to live with me forever. Love each other, be kind to each other, keep your heart open, and I will fill it with my love.

I had asked the Lord to write words of encouragement through me, His open vessel, to you. I am blessed and encouraged by His heartfelt words of love to each one of you. The Lord would like me to also write down two quotes for you, written by Henry Drummond (1851-1897)

"The world is not a play-ground: it is a school room. Life is not a holiday, but an education. And the one eternal lesson for us all is how better we can love!"

"You will find as you look back upon your life that the moments when you have truly lived are the moments when you have done things in the spirit of love."

"Father, I want to thank you for sharing all of this with us. Help each one of us to learn how to love the way you love. Amen!

I believe that this Kingdom Age we are *now* living in on this earth has everything to do with love. It's about being a family who chooses to get along and chooses to learn how to love each other the same way the citizens in Heaven love each other. Dad, I am willing to learn and to keep learning how to love your way and not my way. In Jesus name, Amen.

What about you? Will you join me in this great love adventure? I want all of you to know that in my heart I do love all of you! Which is huge for me because love to me as a child was negative, but God's love changed that and every day His love increases in me. *"Dear friends, let us love one another, for love comes from God. Everyone who loves has been born of God and knows God. Whoever does not love does not know God, because God is love."* 1 John 4:7-8 (NIV)

Encouraging words are important to think about and important to speak but the words must also be followed with action. Jesus always followed His words through with action. There is nothing more frustrating than someone declaring something and then not following through with action. I have learned not to make promises I can't keep and I learned that lesson the hard way. Jesus, my dad, is always present giving me helpful correction and the opportunity to try it again.

Jesus will never leave you nor forsake you as it proclaims to us in Deuteronomy 31:6. On Sunday, April 2, 2017, Jesus encouraged me to run to a small grocery outlet store which was a fifteen-minute drive from where we were living in Arden, North Carolina. This was the third beautiful Mountain Community we had been sent to live in since we arrived in North Carolina on April 24, 2011. We also knew we would be moving again in July of 2017. Jesus is making sure we live in and are familiar with the entire area of our North Carolina promised land. This is the land we have been called to live in, to be His Brides, and to take spiritual dominion over.

When I arrived at the grocery store, I went to unlock a cart. Each cart is secured with a chain and lock. To unlock the chain and free up a cart, one quarter is inserted into a slot in the front of a small black box attached close to the handle of the cart you want to take. Then when you bring the cart back to the cart rack all you have to do is stick the chain from the cart already stored in the rack into the opening of the small black box on the cart you are returning. This releases the quarter to take and use again for your next shopping visit.

So, with my unlocked cart I went shopping. I checked out and left the store to place my groceries into my car. When I reached my car, Jesus told me that someone will need a quarter to unlock a cart. I said "ok." Not only did I still have the quarter inserted in the device on my cart, but I also had a quarter in my purse.

After loading my groceries in my car, I went to return the cart to the rack. As I reached the cart rack, a tired looking Hispanic woman was trying to open her wallet and I said, "Here take my cart." She accepted and smiled as she took my cart and I was encouraged to know she could retrieve the quarter when she was done shopping. I turned and started to walk back to my car when I saw a teenage boy standing close to the entrance door of the store waiting for someone. I saw his mom was walking across the parking lot toward him while trying to open up her wallet. I heard her say to her son, "Do you have a quarter?" He quickly responded no while patting down his pants pockets. She replied with frustration, "I think I only have a nickel."

During this interaction I knew in the spirit this woman was also looking up to God and thinking she needed to find a quarter in her wallet but was not really expecting Him to make one magically appear. As she finished walking across the parking lot while looking in her purse and talking to her son, she stopped and looked up from her wallet and saw me standing with my right arm stretched out holding her needed quarter.

I said, "I have a quarter." As I gave it to her she looked shocked and amazed. She was speechless. Her hoping for a quarter was heard by God and answered. God's perfect timing! I know the angels kept me covered because she was left standing there not really seeing me only knowing that God gave her a quarter. What encouragement the words were to her, "I have a quarter!" I give all the glory to God! I know that the glory of God shines through me, it also shines off from all the angels that travel with me. I love it that way. It's not about me it's all about the Father meeting a need with words of encouragement followed by action.

Dad told me someone would be needing a quarter and I had the pleasure to be that fulfilment *twice,* to two separate women in need. No need is too small for our Father in Heaven. Small is great in the Kingdom of God. I write about the significance of the small in my first book. I encourage you to read it, it was an encouragement for me to write it with the help of the Lord.

I am always encouraged by the reviews from my readers. If I did not have anyone to read what I write, there would be no need to write. It can be uncomfortable to put yourself out there and it is words of encouragement from you that help cheer me on to keep writing. Thank You! I would like to share with you the first two reviews I received after the writing of my very first book detailing my chamber experiences, published in 2012.

"I've been reading your book and have been thoroughly enjoying it. It's really inspiring and encouraging me, aiding me in my walk with Christ. (Alan, N.C.)

"This is an amazing book!! If you want to strive and grow in your relationship with Jesus, I highly recommend this book! When I started reading it, it was hard to put down. I wanted to keep reading about her experiences with Jesus. The way she has written this book makes me feel like I am experiencing it with her. This book has now encouraged me to go out in this world and have my own conversations and experiences with God!! I loved it!! (anonymous, N.C.)

Jesus, bless every one of my readers with a special touch of your love today and I pray that one day you will give me the opportunity to personally meet each and every one of them.

Fourteen

Word Chamber

Every day I hear words spoken to me from heaven, from the one who sits upon His throne. The throne room is a beautiful room filled with words, music, singing, dancing, and the laying down of crowns. All of His children are welcome to participate in all that goes on in His throne room. We are free to lay prostrate before Him. Ask the Father to give you countless throne room experiences while you dwell in your own chamber in heaven.

1 Kings 22:19 (NIV) *"Micaiah said, "Therefore, hear the **word** of the Lord; I saw the Lord sitting on His throne, and all the host of heaven standing by Him on His right and on His left."* One thing I have learned while dwelling in my chamber is that the chamber will expand and grow like the throne room does. The throne room never runs out of room no matter how many want to come in to be with the Father. In my chamber or in the throne

room I always feel like I have a front row seat and I will not miss out on anything.

I remember vividly a time I was up and in my chamber. I didn't see Jesus right away but I knew He was standing right next to me. I felt like I was looking out a window as my eyes started to travel. I knew I was headed towards the throne room. Suddenly, I was above and looking down into the throne room as if I were viewing it from an expansive TV screen. I was not aware of any specific activity in the throne room but I'm sure it was full of activity. I knew Jesus was going to teach me something new and reveal to me a new revelation.

Father was sitting on the throne and I remember seeing His massive figure of light but my eyes were only able to see a side view of God's open mouth. I saw words in English one at a time flowing out from His mouth. Each word was in a beautiful script and each word looked like a wisp of air and each wisp was contained inside a light white swirling color and it was alive. Each word He spoke was alive with movement.

I remember I felt like I had the best seat in the house, front and center. It was my choice to capture God's words into my heart after He spoke them and so I did! I saw and felt each wispy word flow gently right into my heart. They were mine to have and to hold forever, to carry them inside me while on earth or in heaven. The spoken and written words from heaven's throne room are food for our souls *"Taste and see that the Lord is good. Oh, the joys of those who trust in Him!"* Psalm 34:8.

I was then given a new revelation. I was shown by Jesus how all of His children are able to come up into His throne room to receive from our Father new words and capture them, whether they be words for the body of Christ as they meet together or words for the individual child of God. I saw the wisps of words floating, swirling, and filling the throne room as many of His children who make up the body of Christ came up from the earth to receive His words. Each child was being transported to the throne room in their own gigantic clear bubble that looked similar to a bubble from a bubble wand.

As each child of God floated gently inside their own bubble, they were carried into the throne room. When they arrived in the throne room I couldn't see the bubbles anymore I only saw each person. Each child of God stood ready to capture the same words that I saw. Then I saw these words begin to multiply so they could be captured by more children in His body. The words that were not captured continued to swirl and float away from the Throne Room.

The words then began to move through the atmosphere down through the third layer of heaven and continued to move down through the second layer of heaven and into the first layer of heaven, then down to the earth. The words were filling the atmosphere of the Heavens and the earth.

I watched as the words continued to move down through the layers into the core of the earth, consuming and filling the inside layers of the earth until nowhere in all of the earth or in all of heaven was void of the words of the Father. His words are available to be captured by His people on the earth, even people on the earth who have not yet received His son. God's word wisps are spoken by Him and they can be captured and received or rejected at any level in the heavens or in the earth's atmosphere while they are moving, swirling, floating and filling.

After this experience and new revelation, I started hearing or reading in our media, on billboards, or commercials on the TV, on the internet, on you-tube, even in magazines and newspapers words I had seen and heard from the throne room. The words that I had captured from the Father, which were spoken personally to me, began to show up in all of these places.

I was up and in my word chamber and from the throne room Father spoke to me a new two-word wisp, "Hot Spots" which pertains to many of the assignments the Lord has called Jay and I to here on the earth. A few days after I had captured the words, we began to hear or read the same two words repeatedly. For instance, we were taking a casual drive on the highway leading to South Carolina and as we were nearing South Carolina I saw a huge billboard advertisement saying, "Come visit our new Hot Spot in South Carolina." Then in smaller print was written the city which was now the new "Hot Spot."

A few weeks after this, I read on a gas station sign in North Carolina advertising that they were the new "Hot Spot." People should stop in and fill up their gas tank. So, the point is God's spoken words never cease to exist, they continue on forever and bring new life into our hearts. It is our choice at what level we choose to go up and in to capture God's words. For me, I choose to always go right up into the throne room every day, front and center.

Often, the Holy Spirit will alert me that Father is going to speak His new words and I will immediately go up to listen, to capture, and to receive them. Or there will be times when I will ask God "What are your new words from heaven for me today?" I always write them down in my quiet time chamber journal. I never want ignorance to have any place in my heart resulting in His words being ignored. Right now, I can smell bubble gum fill my bedroom. This aroma represents childlike faith. After all, we are His children. No wonder the Holy Bible is known as the Word of God. His spoken words were written for us. Make sure to go up and into the heavens to capture and receive each new word the Father speaks so each word will then be captured into your heart.

"Heaven and earth will disappear, but my Words will remain forever." Matthew 24:35

So be careful little ears what you hear!

I remember these words of a childhood song I sang in Sunday School frequently. It's a simple little tune with powerful words. I am being reminded right now by the Holy Spirit to write down the bible verse James 1:19 *"My dear brothers and sisters, be quick to listen, slow to speak, and slow to get angry."* Whenever I read this scripture it reminds me of who I used to be. Not with one of these thorns in my soul but with all three. I was not quick to listen, I was not slow to speak, and I sure was not slow to get angry. I am a work in progress!

Jesus and I together have made tremendous progress over the years to overcome, to deliver me, and to keep each one of these three thorns out of my soul. But I will also tell you it is a daily process and a constant maintaining to keep them out because they want to sneak back in any way they can. It is a battle but Christ in me wins because when I go into any battle I know that someone must be the victor. I intend that victor to be me! And someone must be defeated and that would be satan!

So, whenever you or I engage in a battle I remind you again, someone must come out the victor, the winner. Never give up the battle, never loose. Remember, satan is the looser and believe me he does not like it when I remind him of that! Always be prepared daily by getting dressed in the morning with these important pieces of attire:

Belt of Truth

Sword of the Spirit

Word of God

Body Armor of Righteousness

Filled with the Holy Spirit & His Glory

Shoes of Peace

Authority in the name of Jesus

Shield of Faith

Know the Power of His blood

Helmet of Salvation

The Hosts of Heaven are available

Fifteen

Host Chamber

"The Angel of the Lord encamps around those who fear Him, and rescues them." Psalm 34:7 (NASB) Angels showing up and making themselves known to myself or my husband is an everyday experience for us. It is natural and comforting to always have each one of them around. I have noticed that the angels who encamp around my husband, myself and my children and their families is increasing in number every day because I simply ask Jesus to increase them. *"Praise Him, all His angels; praise Him, all His heavenly hosts."* Psalm 148:2 (NIV)

Jesus continues to teach me about His created heavenly beings but lately He is teaching me on why He created His hosts, what they look like, and the fact that we can, in Christ, command His hosts. Hosts were created to be the armies of heaven, Revelation 19:14 (NIV) *"And the armies which were in heaven followed*

Him on white horses, wearing pure white linen." They are always available and have been created to help us defeat all enemies!

All we need to do is to *first* ask our God to send to us our very own troop of hosts. Jesus gave us His example to follow in Matthew 26:53 (ESV) *"Do you think that I cannot appeal to my Father, and He will at once send me more than twelve legions of angels?"* Second, is to tell the hosts what to battle and where to go. We can be very specific. 1 Chronicles 21:15 (NIV) *"And God sent an angel to destroy Jerusalem. But as the angel was doing so, the Lord saw it and was grieved because of the calamity and said to the angel who was destroying the people, "Enough! Withdraw your hand," The angel of the Lord was then standing at the threshing floor of Araunah the Jebusite."*

Our command in Christ releases them to be sent out to their battle assignments and when they are finished, they will quickly return back to us to receive the next command. *"Bless the Lord, ye His angels, that excel in strength, that do His commandments, hearkening unto the voice of His word."* Psalm 103:20 (KJB) Don't forget we are to do the works of Christ and even greater works while we live on this earth.

I like to keep my hosts very busy so they will never be bored because I don't think they like being bored. I asked God to show me what they look like and just like that He did. I also asked Him how many do I have? He said I am up to 900 million. God revealed to me that the more Hosts I ask for to send out the more He will send to me. I see them every day when I look up at our sky, His first heaven. Many of His hosts look strange to me. Some of them look like their bodies are made up of large boulders while others are giant in stature, fierce looking and carry sharp fiery glowing spears that are probably double-edged swords. At least that is my interpretation of what I see. Others remind me of the transformer figures, toys my boys liked playing with when they were young. But my favorite hosts are the ones who have the face of a lion. They are stunning!

I am sure I will continue to see many more unique hosts as well as God's other beautiful created celestial beings. Often when I am taking a walk outside, I will look up and God will show me one of His beings. He will then explain to me the being's purpose, why that being was created. Each were created to fulfill a specific purpose. *"For the Lord Almighty has purposed, and who can thwart Him? His hand is stretched out, and who can turn it back?"* Isaiah 14:27 (NIV) and in Revelation 14:6 it reads, *"Then I saw another angel flying in midair, and he had the eternal gospel to proclaim to those who live on the earth---to every nation, tribe, language and people."*

It is fun when God is revealing His new revelations to me. He will purposely open my eyes to see what is going on in the invisible realm. Whatever He opens and makes visible for me to see He often makes it visible for others to see as well. Then they can experience the invisible becoming visible. This frequently happens for me when Jay is experiencing something. I will also get to see what God is revealing to him. His favor is so special, I continually ask for more of it. *"Toward the scorners He is scornful, but to the humble He gives favor."* Proverbs 3:34 (ESV) and Psalms 5:12 (ESV) *"For you bless the righteous, O Lord; you cover him with favor as with a shield"*

I was sitting outside on our back deck on a comfortable patio chair one warm sunny afternoon. It was at the house we were renting in Mills River, North Carolina in 2017. I was asking Father to allow me to see what a spiritual battle really looks like because I was sensing one was going on right at that moment above me in the clouds. The attack was against me. After making my request known I stayed sitting still and focused. I gazed up and I began thinking heavenly thoughts and I began to see the battle in the spiritual realm. That's it, that is all I did! I like simple. I simply like God's Glory Power living inside of me. I believe it is pure holy power and it is infused with His light and with His presence, all wrapped up in one.

It really didn't take long at all for me to notice a massive dark grey cloud that contained a huge black ugly creature inside of it. This ugly creature was filled with just as ugly little demon creatures inside of itself and they were hanging their bodies half way out of this huge ugly creature. I saw all of these demon creatures throwing off from their fingertips these gloomy colored looking waves of energy. They were shooting these waves toward a tremendous white cloud located only a few feet in front of them.

This white cloud was filled with light. It was as many miles wide as it was high. I looked inside the mist and I saw the face of a strange being that resembled a dragon but not like the pictures of dragons we see in story books. I also saw hosts with this dragon and the hosts were standing right next to the dragon face. The hosts were mighty and they could not be moved. I watched as this tremendous white cloud also contained additional hosts. I did not count them. I watched them all move in sync and in precision inside the cloud which seemed to be their transport. The white cloud was changing its direction by moving up and over the huge dark cloud that was filled with the demon creatures. It was as if they were being swallowed up to be carried away.

I blinked and quickly looked again and the sky was at peace. I saw only the beautiful blue sky. Talk about "in the blink of an eye" like scripture says. I am always fascinated at God's creativity and the many strange looking creations He has created and continues to create. All of them are quite incredible and beautiful. They love to obey their God of creation.

I believe Jesus wants us *all* to see them! He is waiting to train *all* of us, His brides, as to how we are to engage into spiritual warfare with His armies of heaven. I love engaging in any spiritual battle. I know He is training and teaching many of His children in the body of Christ who want to learn and are willing to learn His battle strategies. I like the fact that I am and will always be in training and learning from Jesus His new ways to live this powerful Life of the Bride in Him. He is the one who stirs up my heart to expand my mind's thoughts to be His thoughts and my ways to be His ways. I like to stay open for His new revelations to come in to fill my heart and then invade my mind with His way of thinking. When we operate under His battle plans together, we can get the job done. I think of it as Heaven and earth gluing themselves together as one in my life. It is a FUN way to live life!! I get to wake up each day and go to bed each night stuck to Jesus.

"Praise the Lord! Praise the Lord from the heavens! Praise Him from the skies! Praise Him, all His angels! Praise Him, all the armies of heaven! Praise Him, sun and moon! Praise Him, all you twinkling stars! Praise Him, skies above! Praise Him, vapors high above the clouds! Let every created thing give praise to the Lord, for He issued His command, and they came into being.

He established them forever and forever. His orders will never be revoked." Psalm 148:1-6

Sixteen

Confidence Chamber

A definition for the word confidence is; The feeling or belief that one can rely on someone or something; firm trust. Helen Keller wrote by saying, "Self-pity is our worst enemy and if we yield to it, we can never do anything wise in this world." Proverbs 3:26 quotes *"For the Lord will be your confidence, and will keep your foot from being caught."* I agree with both of these quotes. Attaining confidence is a growing process for me because as I become more confident in the Lord and who I am in Christ the more self-pity will not be found inside of me.

I remember early on in our marriage Jay gave me the best advice one day when I was having a pity-party. He said in a loving but firm declaration to me, "Jamie, there comes a time when you need to grow up and get over yourself." And you know, Jay was absolutely right! He knew it was the best advice he could give me because when Jay was in his early to mid-twenties he too decided he needed to grow up and get over himself and he did just that! Now he is an incredible man of God who is so loving, kind, and compassionate. He makes a continuous, conscious effort to think of others before himself. I see Jesus in him. It is good to be people of integrity and I am so glad Jay was not afraid to hurt my feelings by speaking the truth. It really snapped me out of my self-pity and moved me forward into confidence. My confidence continues to mature as I continue to see Jesus living in Jay and His glory power through him 24/7.

The characteristics which make up integrity are; honesty, strong moral principles, moral uprightness, it's a state of being whole and undivided, it is unity. I believe we, the body of Christ, need to get along with each other and when we choose confidence, not self-pity, and make an effort to live in every one of those characteristics of integrity, we move forward until we are easily living in unity as the citizens in heaven are living at this moment! It is a whole new way of life for us, His Body, His Brides, to live in unity right now here on the earth!

When you think about it, we all have direct spiritual access to the Father, Son, and Holy Spirit anytime, anyplace. I encourage you to take the time to go up and into heaven, into your own chamber to be filled with His confidence. Then, come back down to dwell in unity within the body, among all of our brothers and sisters in Christ. Sounds like a great plan to me!

1 Corinthians 12:12-13 (NIV) *"Just as a body, though one, has many parts, but all its many parts form one body, so it is with Christ. For we were all baptized by one Spirit so as to form one body---whether Jews or Gentiles, slave or free---and were all given the one Spirit to drink."*

Ephesians 4:3 (NIV) "Make every effort to keep the unity of the Spirit through the bond of peace."

John 17:23 (NIV) "I in them and you in me—so that they may be brought to complete unity. Then the world will know that you sent me and have loved them even as you have loved me."

Hebrews 4:16 (NASB) "Therefore let us draw near with confidence to the throne of grace, so that we may receive mercy and find grace to help in the time of need."

Proverbs 20:7 "The godly walk with integrity; blessed are their children after them."

Hebrews 10:35 "Do not throw away this confident trust in the Lord, no matter what happens. Remember the great reward it brings you!"

1 Peter 3:8 (NIV) "Finally, all of you, be like-minded,

be sympathetic, love one another, be compassionate and humble."

Seventeen

Promise Chamber

Promise Keeper

Are you a promise keeper or a promise breaker? I think we as humans have kept promises and have broken promises made to each other or to ourselves. I try to always think first and not make promises I know I may not be able to keep. I like to follow through with what I say I will do.

In the book of James, it speaks the exact words to remember when promising anything to anyone. *"But above all, my brothers and sisters, do not swear, either by heaven or by earth or by any other oath, but let your "yes" be yes and your "no" be no, so that you may not fall under condemnation."* James 5:12 (ESV). When we do say "Yes" we really should draw from the Holy Spirit to help us to follow through. These following scriptures encourage us to know what the right action is to take. *"I will not violate my covenant or alter the word that went forth from my lips."* Psalm 89:34 (ESV). The Lord also tells us these words. *"It is the same with my word. I send it out, and it always produces fruit. It will accomplish all I want it to, and it will prosper everywhere I send it. You will live in joy and peace."* Isaiah 55:11-12. Our words spoken in Christ and our words spoken without Christ are powerful and they produce positive or negative results in our lives or in the lives of others. Let me give you a few examples.

In June 2012 I flew to Wisconsin to attend a family event. My oldest son at that time was living in Johnson Creek, and the Lord suggested I stay there. While I was there, I decided to visit a relative who was about an hour and a half north of Johnson Creek. After my visit I returned back to my son's home and decided to get to bed at a reasonable time because I would be flying back home to North Carolina early afternoon the following day. I was glad that the airport was only about a twenty-minute drive from their home.

When I packed my bags that evening and looked for my driver's license, I realized I had left it up north. It was the only picture ID I had with me and I could not board the plane without it. I quickly called to make sure it was left there and would be kept safe. I woke up at the crack of dawn to get myself ready and placed my luggage in the trunk of my rental vehicle. I wanted to make sure I would have plenty of time to drive up north and back to the airport.

When I was about to leave the house the tornado sirens went off, so I quickly alerted my son but because he is an air traffic controller he decided to stay in bed as he had to get enough sleep for his next shift. It was sort of funny because I realized I was acting like he was still twelve years old and he needed me to keep him safe. Well, I apologized to him and I went out on the back deck of the house. As I stood outside, I looked at the sky and sure enough up to my left was a big black storm cloud and one funnel had streamed down from the cloud.

I, as a bride of Christ, have power over the weather so I pointed to that funnel cloud and I commanded it in Jesus name to go right back up into that cloud and disappear because I needed to leave and get back in time for my flight. That is exactly what happened!!! I watched that funnel go right back up into that big black storm cloud and the whole cloud dissolved. I yelled out, "Thank You Jesus!" I then left and returned from up north in plenty of time to catch my flight home.

I believe it is important to remember that within ourselves we are powerless. It is only Christ in us who has the glory power through us to do all things that are good. It is the evil one of darkness who acts on a person's negative words and will make those words come into being and will set up a false future of events in a person's life.

At times, we may hear a person make a comment like, "I am sick and tired of being sick and tired." What can happen when this is said? You got it, their bodies usually are sick and tired because they say it so much that they are really cursing themselves. Our negative words, or negative thoughts, or even negative words read or written down on paper over and over and over again can give darkness the power to make it happen. But the awesome news is... Jesus can rescue us and teach us in our chambers how to speak positive words and how to combat the negative to make them null and void. Jesus can take our negative and put that negative funnel right back up in that storm cloud and make it dissolve.

I think it is important to remember life and death are in the tongue as is cursing and blessing. We must always be careful not to speak negative about anyone. I often see believers who say or post on social media negative words or negative videos of people who they feel are wrong or view them as their enemies. Then their next post is glorifying God and His son Jesus, or His Holy Spirit. Scripture does not tell us to do this at all. We must not have a double standard. We must not use words or actions to bash anyone even when it comes to politics, simply stating the facts is appropriate.

The Lord is really good at teaching us to stand and speak in the Spiritual realm. This is the place where all things must be broken first and then we will be able to see the results manifest on the earth. We must always be careful because Michael the Archangel would not even accuse satan! *"Yet Michael the archangel, when contending with the devil he disputed about the body of Moses durst not bring against him a railing accusation, but said, The Lord rebuke thee."* Jude 1:9 (KJB). I have seen Michael a few times and he is a mighty, fierce, and chiseled looking angel. We MUST, like Jay always reminds me, THINK before we speak.

I like to give the Holy Spirit permission to always call me on the carpet if I mess up. When I think, speak or do something inappropriate, I can immediately renounce it, ask for forgiveness, and be open to receiving His help in keeping the words I speak, my thoughts and my actions as a good representative of Jesus. *"And whatever you do or say, let it be as a representative of the Lord Jesus, all the while giving thanks through Him to God the Father."* Colossians 3:17. It is good to have a voice and even better to speak with words from the Father. Heaven's words spoken through me and you will be a mighty sound on this earth that will destroy darkness.

Eighteen

Kingdom Chamber

Jesus first came into the world as a Savior but when He comes again, He will come as a conquering KING! He is our King and I believe His Kingdom age began in the year 2012. I do not know how long this Kingdom age will last before the perilous time begins. He has not revealed that to me yet but I do know that we, His believers, His body, His chosen ones, His brides, have the choice to step into this kingdom age. And, the sooner the better! The King, through each one of us, will rise up to take spiritual dominion over all the earth in every sector on the earth whether it be inside or outside the church body. It is the time for His glorious glory power, His light, His presence in each one of us to rise up as He leads and directs us. *"Far above all rule and authority and power and dominion, and above every name that is named, not only in this **age** but also in the one to come."* Ephesians 1:21 (ESV).

I feel strongly that it is time to unify, to allow our God given talents and gifts to shine. It is time to rise up and dive into all the various platforms that the Lord leads you and me into! We succeed! It is now the time to begin to live as one in the spiritual realm, as we live and move in this earthly realm as the remnant bride of Christ, His warriors, supernaturally, around the clock, twenty-four-seven! My family and I have taken a huge step and jumped in. I encourage each one of you to jump in with us so you will never be lagging behind to the point where you can't seem to catch up. It is a choice we each need to make, and it is an easy choice. Just say **Yes** and keep going up and into the kingdom chamber. Our King will give you all the details you need to know. Your Savior, your King is waiting for you to ask Him to fill you continually with His Glorious Glory Power, His light, and His presence. It is the new way to live, His way through you.

Glorious Portals

It is amazing to me when I read in scriptures about the wonders of God and Heaven, especially when I find verses that explain exactly what the portals of heaven look like. All of us get to read about the times when God would open up the heavens so his children could see deeper and more intimately into His world in Heaven. *"On July 31 of my thirtieth year, while I was with the Judean exiles beside the Kebar River in Babylon, the heavens were opened to me, and I saw visions of God."* Ezekiel 1:1. *"Then I saw heaven opened, and a white horse was standing there. And the one sitting on the horse was named Faithful and True."* Revelation 19:11. *"Then He said, "The truth is, you will all see heaven open and the angels of God going up and down upon the Son of Man."* John 1:51.

When the heavens are opened to us, we will see! Definitions for the word portal include the following: A gateway, a doorway or a door, entry or a door entrance, a way in. A portal is also a grand and imposing entrance and it is also a site that the owner positions as an entrance to other sites on the internet. An iron or steel bent for bracing a framed structure. These definitions of the word portal are ways into something new and leads into something that has been opened and gives the ability to see, to obtain, and to experience.

I believe a heavenly portal is a real spiritual opening where someone can walk out of or walk into and it provides protection while going up or coming down as well as traveling from one place to another. I believe a portal can travel ahead of us to clear the way. I believe God can send us provisions through a portal. It is an opening where we are able to see the activities that are going on in the spirit; past, present or future.

I have seen a portal in heaven in a place that I call the citizens room. Here the citizens of heaven can look into a portal that looks to me like a tremendous tv/movie screen. They can look and see special events in their loved one's lives on the earth or watch as God moves His power through them on their assignments. *"Therefore, since we are surrounded by such a great cloud of witnesses, let us throw off everything that hinders and the sin that so easily entangles, and let us run with perseverance the race marked out for us."* Hebrews 12:1 (NIV). I also talk about the citizens' room and other spiritual things I have seen on my website.

In scripture the portals are described as open doors, open windows, open heavens, open skies, open gates to name just a few. All are protected openings. A portal connects us for easy access. They are the openings needed to give us the ability to do God's work. 1 Corinthians 16:9 *"For there is a wide-open door for a great work here, and many people are responding. But there are many who oppose me."* Isaiah 60:11 says, *"Your gates will stay open around the clock to receive the wealth of many Lands."* In Malachi 3:10 the Lord tells Malachi this; *"Bring all the tithes into the storehouse so there will be enough food in my Temple. If you do,"* says the Lord Almighty, *"I will open the windows of heaven for you. I will pour out a blessing so great you won't have enough room to take it in! Try it! Let me prove it to you!"* Now these are the kind of doors, gates, and windows I want as my portals!

Portals are invisible and portals can be made visible even to the point where you can film them. That is what I did. I have taken video and I snapped pictures.

On March 2, 2018 I was sitting on my bed in our bedroom and I had just come down from my chamber. I decided to get up and walk into our kitchen to make a hot beverage. The house we were renting at that time had a large living room with a wall of glass windows and a large patio door for easy access to a deck. The deck was high off the ground and it looked out onto our backyard. We had a peaceful view of the narrow Mills River running through our backyard which was a popular river for fly fishing, kayaking and tubing. It was fun to watch people float past the backyard of our home while enjoying the view of the mountain ranges.

I was looking out the window as I was standing next to our kitchen counter. As I was looking out to our backyard, movement caught my eye. I saw something hovering over our deck that looked to me like white waves of a large piece of material that was being rippled by the wind and it seemed to be hanging in midair. I grabbed my cell phone and started to capture a video of the waves. I noticed the wavy motion had decreased where I could not see it anymore. In its place it looked like a ladder going up to heaven. The ladder did not have any rungs on it to climb up. It was a beautiful pink glistening color and near the bottom and to the left of the ladder I saw round gold rings appear.

I moved my cell phone to capture another ladder identical to the first but my phone was not able to capture it so I moved my phone back to continue filming the first ladder. After I had stopped capturing the video. I continued to look at our deck and I noticed a cloudy substance appeared and it was suspended in the air over the middle of the deck. I took a picture of it and started to capture another video of this cloudy substance. As I recorded the cloudy substance, I noticed it was turning into the face of a lion! It was the face of a Host Angel. As I kept recording, I began to notice that several gold rings began to appear and they took on a shape that reminded me of a tunnel, as if I was looking up and inside of a tornado. The tunnel/tornado was reaching up and down and it seemed to consume almost our whole deck.

My portal was connected from heaven to earth and touching down on the middle of our deck. In the center of this gold ringed tunnel it looked to me like there were two large solid gold circles suspended in the air. One gold circle looked to be as if it were a round door placed on the floor and the other circle was the same size but standing upright as if it were a door on the wall of this portal. The two round doors reminded me of two areas you could stand or sit on. All the while in my mind I am talking to God and asking Him if this is what I was discerning it to be? He told me that yes it was a portal from heaven and it belonged to me. God allowed me to not only see my portal but to film it. My portal came from heaven to earth and it was here at our home displaying itself to me on our back deck!

The picture I snapped of my gold portal turned out great as did the two videos I captured with my cell phone. I sent Jay, a few of my children, and two other relatives the video. Later the next day as I viewed my portal video, I continued to see more of the activity that was going on inside my portal. A beautiful white winged angel in a long flowing gown looked to be dancing in the middle of the portal along with six or more additional angels all dancing while moving their wings back and forth.

As I had moved the camera upward to capture the top of the portal rings, I saw one white angel sitting on a tree branch just hanging out while dangling his legs. Angels love to have fun and dance. They are very entertaining and comical at times. These are my angels assigned to me and they are waiting inside of my portal for God's directions as to how and when they will be released to help me. They are the ones who will deliver God's gifts from heaven to me. I am sure in the days to come I will know more of their assignments as they start showing up in my life in unexpected and mysterious ways.

When I saw my portal in person it had such a beautiful solid gold color within each and every ring that glistened with a substance I will never find on this earth. It is precious gold from heaven. It was fascinating to see how each ring that was extending up toward heaven appeared to change from a gold color into a white glowing color and they were moving with a gentle swaying motion as if each ring had a life of its own. Each ring was praising God. Our God is Amazing! And on March 2, 2019, exactly one year later, my gold portal showed up again outside on our yard and right in front of our bedroom window. I captured another video of it on my cell phone. I pray one day I will be able to show it to you. People who have seen it are amazed as it makes heaven and earth become one in their lives. His Glory is spectacular! I want to thank you Father for giving each one of us our very own Golden portals. I love living in your kingdom age and I love going up and into my Kingdom chamber to be with my King.

Proclaim with me Psalm 24:7,

"OPEN UP, ANCIENT GATES!

OPEN UP, ANCIENT DOORS!

AND LET THE KING OF GLORY ENTER"

Nineteen

Understand Chamber

"His disciples asked Him what the story meant. He replied, "You have been permitted to understand the secrets of the Kingdom of God." Luke 8:9

When I can understand what I hear or what I read I am able to apply it to my life. I am the type of person that I need to understand it fully. It's important for me to "get it." I will keep seeking out the Father until I fully understand. This is how it is for me in anything I attempt to work at because if I can *first* understand it then I can give it my best and put my whole heart into it and do the best I can. 2 Timothy 2:15 (NIV) explains my best like this... *"Do your Best to present yourself to God as one approved, a worker who does not need to be ashamed and who correctly handles the word of truth."*

Some people, like Jay and my children, seem to have such an incredible ability to understand so much quicker than I do. Many of them have photographic memories, I do not!

I know what the bible says. I love to digest every single word as if I am eating food. I guess I love to devour it. I love to search and find bible verses, but some people can quote verses effortlessly. I myself have memorized only a few bible verses word for word. I know people who can rattle off bible verses from memory or have memorized verses through repetition by singing them in songs or playing bible memory games when they were children.

Many years ago, I set a goal for myself to memorize as many bible verses as I could. Day after day I would find a scripture verse that was near to my heart and spend time in the evening memorizing it until I could say it word for word. But the next morning when I would wake up wanting to quote the verse from memory it was gone! Finally, after a few days of this I decided to ask God why? Why is it I struggle to memorize scripture?

I will never forget His loving response to me as He reminded me of something he revealed to me several years prior through a short video teaching but that I had long forgotten about. He said, "Jamie, I didn't call you to memorize scripture, I called you to Live it!" I remember feeling peace and the pressure I had placed upon myself was lifted. God then started to share with me that the Holy Spirit within me has a great memory and He will always bring important truth to my mind to share with others even if it is quoting bible verses word for word or paraphrasing.

He then brought back to my memory several assignments He and I had been on. I remembered quoting scripture right at the exact moment the person needed to hear God's words to console them. It is a comforting reality for me to know that every word of scripture I have read and digested from His Holy Bible is locked deep inside my memory. It is stored in my mind safe and sound.

When I am led by the spirit to share bible verses with others, the Holy Spirit will indeed bring the verses up from my memory to speak them or to write them down. He will reveal to me what scripture will have the most impact on someone's life. The Holy Spirit will always keep safe His scriptures inside of me and inside of you. They are countless memories that are locked up and stored away just waiting for the proper time when they are needed to be brought back out. Here are two great scripture verses to read and to lock safe in our memories to be unfolded by the Holy Spirit as needed... *"The unfolding of your words gives light; it gives understanding to the simple."* Psalm 119:130 (NIV) and *"For the Lord gives wisdom; from His mouth comes knowledge and understanding."* Proverbs 2:6 (NIV)

I believe the word understanding is important to the

Father while we are in His Chamber of Understanding it's a necessary place to dwell in every second of every day. Now that is something I will always remember!

"Trust in the Lord with all your heart and lean not on your own understanding." Proverbs 3:5 (NIV)

Twenty

Holy Spirit Chamber

I remember a conversation I had with a close relative who was upset that I loved Jesus. I remember being at a large family event and as we were talking this person bluntly came out and said to me, "There are so many translations of the bible that you can't believe any of it." This relative believed there was a God but did not believe the bible was relevant. It was only a book so why read it. It was not trustworthy. I was a new believer at that time and I was taken back at the anger that was directed at the one I loved and had a close relationship with. I have learned throughout the years that many church going people claiming to believe in the Holy Trinity, feel the same way. Many of them are doubtful concerning the validity of the bible even after they have graduated from a faith-based college. So.... what is missing here?

I believe what is missing is simply the true belief,

the true foundation, the true reality of who the Holy Spirit is and what He actually does. He is the third person in the God head. He, the counselor, was sent by the Father because Jesus asked Him to send the Holy Spirit to be with, to completely fill, and to never leave a new believer. This promise is found in John 14:16,17 *"And I will ask the Father, and He will give you another Counselor, who will never leave you. He is the Holy Spirit, who leads into all truth. The world at large cannot receive Him, because it isn't looking for Him and doesn't recognize Him. But you do, because He lives with you now and later will live in you."* The Holy Spirit is filled with revelation and with power! That is why after a person repents of their sins and accepts what Jesus did on the cross for them, it is also important for the person to confess with their mouth and to simply ask Jesus to come live in their heart! Then the person's heart will be born-again and filled, with His love. Jesus promised that the Holy Spirit will come to be with the new believer.

It is also important for any believer to ask the Holy Spirit to come to live inside of them and to be filled up with His glory power! Why not receive it all and start out fully loaded! The Holy Spirit is **TRUTH.** *"But when the Father sends the Counselor as my representative---and by the counselor I mean the Holy Spirit---He will teach you everything and will remind you of everything I myself have told you."* John 14:26.

The Holy Spirit reveals to us God's truth by helping us understand each and every word written in the bible. Yes, there are many different translations of the Bible but we must ask Him, the Holy Spirit, to help us find a good translation. The Holy Spirit will ignite every word to come alive and be relevant in our daily lives. He will teach us how to speak out the Father's words so they will be used as a double-edged sword. He will teach us to keep our hearts cleansed and our spirits holy as we destroy all the enemies that attack us. *"For the word of God is alive and active. Sharper than any double- edged sword, it penetrates even to dividing soul and spirit, joints and marrow, it judges the thoughts and attitudes of the heart."* Hebrews 4:12 (NIV)

We also need to remember that the Holy Spirit is receiving His information from Jesus who is standing at the right hand of the Father. John chapter 16:14 tells us *"He (Holy Spirit) will bring me glory by revealing to you whatever he receives from me (Jesus)."* The Holy Spirit has never let me down. He helps me to understand what I don't understand. He will also reveal to me what is going on in-between the lines. Let me give you a few examples.

The Holy Spirit and I were reading together a story in Luke 17:11-19 and it was about Jesus when He was traveling to Jerusalem… *"Now on His way to Jerusalem, Jesus traveled along the boarder between Samaria and*

Galilee. As He was going into a village, ten men who had leprosy met Him. They stood at a distance and called out in a loud voice, "Jesus, Master, have pity on us!" When He saw them, He said, "Go, show yourselves to the priests." And as they went, they were cleansed. One of them, when he saw he was healed, came back, praising God in a loud voice. He threw himself at Jesus' feet and thanked Him----and he was a Samaritan. Jesus asked, "Were not all ten cleansed? Where are the other nine? Was no one found to return and give praise to God except this foreigner?" Then He said to him. "Rise and go: your faith has made you well."

After I read these verses a few times I wanted to know more of what happened because I sensed there was more to this story. I will often ask specific questions and address them to the Holy Spirit. I began to discuss this story in detail. I asked the Holy Spirit what happened to the other nine lepers that were healed and didn't come back to say thank you? The Holy Spirit then began to reveal some hidden truths in this story from in-between the lines.

The leper who was a Samaritan was on his way to see the priest to be granted by the priest that he is now clean and could return back into the community to live. But as he was walking and realized he was healed he came running back to *first* thank Jesus, then go to see the priest! The Holy Spirit then revealed to me that because this man came back to give glory and praise to God for his healing, this man maintained his healing! But the other nine, who also went off to see the priest, also realized they were healed but none of them returned to give praise and glory to God. They went on their merry way.

The Holy Spirit revealed to me that those other nine who went on without returning to give glory to God lost their healing after a while. They all contracted leprosy again except for the one because he returned to thank Jesus. I absolutely understood how important faith really is in a person's life and the power of faith through the Holy Spirit who was teaching me in-between the lines.

Another example I want to share was when my three boys were very young. It was at a time when I was near the end of a sad separation and divorce with their father. I asked Jesus a question, I asked "Why did you allow me to have these three beautiful boys when you knew it would end like this?" My answer came many years later when I had been married to Jay for ten years.

I remember I was praying for my second son because he was on his first tour of duty in Iraq. I remember opening up my bible and the Holy Spirit led me to read about Leah and Rachel, the two wives of Jacob. And as I was reading the Holy Spirit revealed to me the answer to my question from many years prior about my boys. God's written words of love and truth healed my heart as I began to read Genesis 29:31-34. Here was the answer to my question of why I have these three beautiful boys; *"But because Leah was unloved, the Lord let her have a child, while Rachel was child-less. So Leah became pregnant and had a son. She named him Reuben, for she said, "The Lord has noticed my misery, and now my husband will love me." She soon became pregnant again and had another son. She named him Simeon, for she said, "The Lord heard that I was unloved and has given me another son." Again she became pregnant and had a son. She named him Levi, for she said, "Surely now my husband will feel affection for me, since I have given him three sons!"* These words of being unloved turned into three beautiful bundles of LOVE. His everlasting love keeps coming because God, in His love, gave Jay and I more love by adding a beautiful daughter into our lives. My love was extended to four times the love! And it still keeps on coming!

Jay is my husband who loves me, and we all are loved by the Father who created each one of us to love and to be loved. It is so important to read the bible with the help of the Holy Spirit because He is so good at unlocking all the truth and understanding we need to be successful in living a life filled up with God's everlasting love and then pouring it out to all people everywhere we go.

Now I would like to share a last example going into greater depth of the greatness of the Holy Spirit and His mighty power of truth and understanding. Years ago, in 2012, I was reading Luke chapter two which tells the time when Jesus was a child growing up in Nazareth. When I came to verses 39-40 it said, *"When Joseph and Mary had done everything required by the Law of the Lord, they returned to Galilee to their own town of Nazareth. And the child grew and became strong: He was filled with wisdom, and the grace of God was upon Him."*

I began to think about Jesus as a child and some of the things a little boy might like to play at that time in history. So I asked Jesus, "What kind of games did you like to play as a child?" Right after I asked this the Holy Spirit took me in the spirit and traveled my spirit back with Him to when Jesus was a young boy. The next thing I knew, the Holy Spirit and I were standing on a thin and narrow street in Nazareth. It was Jesus' childhood hometown and we were observing a young boy around the age of 8 or 9. He was playing a game with a small group of children, boys and girls between the ages of four and seven.

I watched as this boy had gentle sparkling eyes, a radiant smile and love was glowing off from him as he was kicking a stone. I then realized it was a stone kicking game and this boy was Jesus. The boy, Jesus, made sure everyone had a turn and He made sure everyone had fun. There was a lot of laughter on each smiling face but what was fun to observe was that the boy Jesus made sure everyone won in the game when it was their turn to kick. No one lost. Each child was a winner! Jesus' favorite game or at least one of them is called "Kicking the Stone." No wonder when we move back home to heaven Jesus will write our new name on a stone and then hand it to us or.... kick it to us? He loves fun games and laughter!

As soon as I witnessed the answer to my question I was back sitting on my bed and I felt completely loved. The Holy Spirit is power, and He is great at traveling. He loves it when we come along with Him, especially when we ask Him to take us. We must remember God is eternal. He is in control of time; past, present, and future. God can travel anywhere on His or our timelines. Remember He created time; yet in heaven there is no time. In heaven we will be able to view all the wonderful events from our entire lifetime on this earth as well as Jesus' time on the earth from birth, to the cross, to death, to hell, to resurrection, to ascension and everything in-between; plus more than we could ever imagine. Without a doubt, heaven is a wonderful place. You can also ask God to allow the Holy Spirit to take you up to heaven for a visit or to travel around in time anytime you want. I do! Heaven is a great place to visit!

As I've said many times before, the Holy Spirit will also bring you up and into your own chamber to be with Jesus. It is an actual chamber, a place built with you in mind to come up and into. All you need to do is ask Him. Remember the Holy Spirit is power. He has come to dwell in you and fill you with Himself, so you can live supernaturally as His bride, living in His Love and Power. We will be on fire and this earth will never be the same again as we, His body, rise up, move forward, and live like Jesus did on this earth. I am an open vessel who has done the works that Jesus has done. I am now stepping into doing His greater works because the Holy Spirit is teaching me how to do that in His truth and in His understanding and in His Power. And You can too!

"The truth is, anyone who believes in me will do the same works I have done, and even greater works, because I am going to be with the Father. You can ask for anything in my name, and I will do it, because the work of the Son brings glory to the Father. Yes, ask anything in my name, and I will do it!" John 14:12-14.

I believe these verses are of tremendous value and is the reason the Holy Spirit has led me three times now to include them in this book for us to read and re-read. They are essential to operate in as we are living the life of the Bride right now. It is critical for others to see heaven and earth operating as one in our lives! The whole earth will see His signs and wonders demonstrated through us in His love day after day after day so they will know that He Is God! *"You are witnesses that I Am God, says the Lord. From eternity to eternity I Am God. No one can oppose what I do. No one can reverse my actions."* Isaiah 43:12-13. Never Stop Asking! I love this first sentence in Matthew 7:7 ***"Keep on asking, and you will be given what you ask for."***

Twenty-One

Dominion Chamber

Father, Son and Holy Spirit, the three in one, has perfect control over absolutely everything that has been created, is being created and is yet to be created. God has created us in their likeness; Father, Son and Holy Spirit and has given you and I spiritual dominion! This is absolutely mind boggling to me. I take spiritual dominion very seriously!

Genesis 1:26 (KJB) *"And God said, "Let us make man in Our Image, after Our Likeness; and let them have Dominion over the fish of the sea, and over the fowl of the air, and over the cattle, and over all the earth, and over every creeping thing that creepeth upon the earth."*

God has given to each one of us dominion over all that swims, all that flies, all that walks, all that creeps upon the earth. The Latin word for dominion is dominus, meaning Master. We have been given permission by God to be Masters. Are we doing this the way God wants us to?

All of these various animals; fowl, fish and sea creatures, all the creeping things deserve our respect and care and we should not purposely abuse them. I do know that the animals we love, or at least a replica of them, go to heaven when they die. I know they can talk in heaven so take good care of them here on the earth and love them as much as Jesus does. If you wonder about hunting a wild animal for sport, to be a trophy to be admired as it hangs on a wall, I would suggest you "Ask Jesus." He will tell you what He thinks about that, He will reveal to you in scripture the different animals He created and each one's purpose.

I will never forget the day in 2017 when the veterinarian told me our little chihuahua, Lola, was in severe pain because of a degenerative disk disease. She was given pain killers to ease her pain but the pain would not ease. I took her home and talked with Jesus to ask Him if He was going to heal her like he had healed one of my pets in the past.

I had a small dog many years earlier who broke her leg and Jesus healed her little leg while the x-rays were being taken. I stood praying quietly next to the open door of the x-ray room and I realized the staff and the veterinarian were confused because all of them knew her little leg was broken the minute they took her from me to examine her leg. It was fun listening to their conversation as the doctor became upset with his staff for not giving my small dog a proper x-ray so he did the x-ray himself. I smiled because I knew minutes prior to the first x-ray that doctor Jesus fixed her broken leg.

But this time I knew it was His choice to take my little Lola to heaven. After a few days Jay and I knew the decision we needed to make for Lola. Tanique and I took her to her last appointment. We were alone with Lola in the small exam room to say our goodbyes. Lola lay on her stomach on the table and as I crouched down to look into her eyes, I immediately felt a glorious presence come into the examining room and stand on the other side of the table. Tanique was also aware of this and together we witnessed something so amazing about the incredible love Jesus has for all of His creatures.

As I looked into Lola's big beautiful eyes, I could see the tremendous pain she was feeling. I could also see the love she had for me in her eyes. I was Lola's "person." She always liked being with me. As I began to gently stroke her face, I spoke to her in a soft voice as the Holy Spirit was leading me to say, "A man is going to come and get you and His name is Jesus and I want you to go with Him. He is going to take you to heaven. You will have fun there and you will never be in pain again. And one day, I will come to be with you and we will live together forever in my mansion."

After I said this Tanique and I knew Lola understood every single word I said. Lola looked at me and we felt the glorious presence come over to the side of the table where I was still in a crouched down position. A tremendous peace filled the room. We watched as Lola's eyes moved to look at the presence who was now crouching down next to me and it was indeed Jesus. Lola moved her eye's back to look at me. I tenderly said to Lola, "You can go now with Jesus." Lola's eyes were full of love and began to glisten with tears. Then in the spirit we watched something so beautiful as the life inside her was tenderly picked up by Jesus. He cradled little Lola in His arms, turned, and she was gone traveling to her new home in heaven. *"Not even a sparrow, worth only half a penny, can fall to the ground without your Father knowing it."* Matthew 10:29.

The doctor came in to see if it was time and we said, "Yes" and we both had big smiles on our faces. I am sure the doctor thought that was strange but then without first checking Lola the doctor gave her the injection, but we knew she had already left. Tanique and I smiled at each other and with tears of joy welling up in our eyes I gave Lola a kiss on the bridge of her nose one last time. Tanique and I left, giving God the glory and celebrating the fact that His creation never dies!

The blood of Jesus has conquered sin and death so that we who have been made in His image and likeness, can choose to accept the blood of the lamb and live life to its fullest on the earth and then move on to continue living a forever life in Heaven!

About one year after Jesus took Lola home to live with Him, I was at my home walking down our hallway and in-between one of my steps I felt the spiritual atmosphere around me shift. It felt like time had suddenly stopped. Before me, as if floating in the air, I saw my beautiful little Lola jumping high in the air as she was running through a field of the most gorgeous, elegant flowers I had ever seen. I could hear her laughing and talking with the flowers. It seemed as if each and every flower was talking and laughing too. They were very much alive. It was astounding! Scripture says this, *"However, as it is written: What no eye has seen, what no ear has heard, and what no human mind has conceived---the things God has prepared for those who love Him."* 1 Corinthians 2:9 (NIV)

Do you Love Him? I know I sure do! I am grateful for His mercy and for His grace. *"For sin shall not have Dominion over you; for ye are not under the law, but under grace."* Romans 6:14 (KJB)

Grace is for everyone

Grace doesn't give you the right to sin

Grace gives you the reason not to sin

Grace is powerful but the evil enemy has been

stirring inside the church body, filling people with the attitude that grace covers sin and that they are safe in their sin. Let me give you an example. This will be the short version of a very long and complicated assignment from God for Jay and I.

This assignment truly taught us how a false grace spirit likes to operate. Jay and I were involved in a four-year business/friendship with a man who loved the Lord and was spirit filled. The Lord had blessed him with a gift, a very unique and one of a kind invention that was definitely going to corner a niche in its particular market. It would produce great financial wealth for him, his partner, for us and for other employees who would be involved early on in this new business venture.

This new one-of-a-kind invention came directly from the throne room of God. It was definitely impacting this industry and was indeed beginning to gain popularity in the market where it would be sold. The invention was being shown at trade shows and the word began to spread with potential orders beginning to flood in. It was gaining notoriety in the industry. It was gaining fame and glory. God was indeed leading the way until this man began making wrong choices in his personal life which then started having great adverse effects on the business. The hand of God started to lift up and off of this man but God did not lift His hand off Jay and I.

The Lord quickly began revealing to Jay that this

man was trapped under a false grace. It started off slowly but then continued to grow inch by inch until this false grace opened up a place in his heart for an unclean spirit to enter. The filling progressed to where he lived with another woman while he was still married to his wife. This man would speak often about God's grace, but he was believing the lie that grace would cover his sin no matter what and he did not end the sin behavior. His attitude was God understands his sin.

Jay and I were very close to this situation and the Lord asked us to do something we couldn't understand. He asked us to love him unconditionally, to stand by him and to battle in the spiritual realm for him, his wife, his children, his employees, his friends and for the woman he openly lived with. We were in a fierce battle for souls to be snatched back! We readily obeyed and did exactly what God asked us to do! The last two years of the four-year battle were indeed the hardest. We spent those two years defending his right to control this invention, and his business, in court proceedings alongside this man. The Lord would *not* allow Jay or I to find any kind of employment during that time which was difficult but God provided for us.

At the end of the court battle this man did win back his invention because it came from God. It belonged to God and the enemy could not take it from God. To our knowledge the invention is standing still and has not yet moved forward. Only God knows what He has planned for this new invention. Maybe this man will get another chance at it or maybe God will give this invention to another.

We pray blessings upon them all because there is one thing I know about God; He can turn everything around in a heartbeat! He truly is a God of restoration because He is love! And because He wins every battle! We need to always remember God has given us authority to rule in the spiritual realm in the heavenlies and to take dominion on the earth.

"Thou madest him to have Dominion over the works of thy hands; thou hast put all things under his feet." Psalm 8:6 (KJB)

"To Him be glory and Dominion for ever and ever. Amen!" 1 Peter 5:11 (KJB)

Twenty-Two

Giving Chamber

"I want it to be a willing gift, not one given under pressure." This is what I read in 2 Corinthians 9:5. As I continue to read verses 7-9 it is made very clear to me what our Father in heaven thinks about giving. *"You must each make up your own mind as to how much you should give. Don't give reluctantly or in response to pressure. For God loves the person who gives cheerfully. And God will generously provide all you need. Then you will always have everything you need and plenty left over to share with others. As the Scriptures say, "Godly people give generously to the poor. Their good deed will never be forgotten."*

I believe everything we have belongs to God. He is entrusting us with His gift of finances to manage them through His gift of sound wisdom. He desires to gift us with both finances and wisdom. Our philosophy on giving is we simply ask God to decide, "How much do we keep and how much do we give away?" God is awesome at managing His finances through us, His children, because He always knows exactly what to do with them. We regularly ask for sound wisdom along with incredible business sense.

I remember a time when I was up and in my giving chamber. I was asking Jesus to give me His thoughts on tithing because I felt it was often being abused within the body of Christ. He explained to me that He looks more at the condition of the heart when a person is giving to fill a financial need. We must take into account that we are currently under the New covenant and not the Old.

We read in the old testament what being under the *law*, the old covenant, was like. There are many scriptures that tell us about the giving of tithes and the different percentage amounts the Israelites were required to give, when they were to give them and where they were to give them. They needed guidance from God and He taught them to be responsible in their giving to God from their bountiful crops, resources and coins. I believe we need to have a cheerful heart with the attitude, "I am willing to give it all."

Jay and I do not focus on a ten percent tithe because for us it binds us. We love to be open givers with hands giving out whatever the Lord stirs in our hearts to give. If a need is presented to us where we feel pressured, reluctant or obligated to give, we immediately go up and in to our giving chambers to discuss the situation with our Father. He will immediately tell us what to do. Another scripture I love is this; *"Give whatever you can according to what you have. If you are really eager to give, it isn't important how much you are able to give. God wants you to give what you have, not what you don't have. Of course, I don't mean you should give so much that you suffer from having too little. I only mean that there should be some equality. Right now you have plenty and can help them. Then at some other time they can share with you when you need it. In this way, everyone's needs will be met."* 2 Corinthians 8:11-15.

I believe it is dangerous to flirt around with an attitude of *giving to get*. When we give through a kind act to someone and have the attitude that there needs to be a payback we are living dangerously. We all need to keep our hearts in check because if any of us give without a cheerful heart then I believe it is best to stop, hold back, and wait. All our deeds of giving will be put through the fire.

The Holy Spirit is now bringing something up from my memory. It was an experience where I was standing with Jesus in my chamber and it was during a time that He was teaching me about giving. I remember I saw a tremendous fire burning and it reminded me of an alter of fire. As Jesus and I looked into the fire I saw what appeared to be acts of good deeds inside the fire. I watched as one good deed after another was being burned up in the fire as if it were going through the fire on a conveyor belt. I could almost feel how hot the flames were while they were burning, and each good deed was being engulfed with flames. I was then a bit startled as I watched because one good deed jumped up and out of the fire onto the ground close to our feet. I looked and saw this good deed had been purified and transformed into a beautiful sparkling jewel right before my eyes.

I kept watching and began to see several giving deeds of finances that appeared to be very good deeds. As the flames burned, I saw that all the finances burnt up in the fire and quickly became black ashes. The black ashes disintegrated right before my eyes. I looked at Jesus and I know He saw the look of shock on my face. I was surprised by what appeared to be very good financial gifts that were not so good and they all burned up. To me they were lost jewels that didn't make it through the fire, and I felt sad. I am not saying that believers who have any of their deeds burned up will not be saved. I guess what I am saying is that to me, the givers will come up short on jewels that should have jumped out of the fire to land by their feet due to their heart attitude.

It was quite a while after this visual lesson when

the Holy Spirit led me to read these scripture verses to reveal a deeper teaching from what I saw that day; *"But there is going to come a time of testing at the judgment day to see what kind of work each builder has done. Everyone's work will be put through the fire to see whether or not it keeps its value. If the work survives the fire, that builder will receive a reward. But if the work is burned up, the builder will suffer great loss. The builders themselves will be saved, but like someone escaping through a wall of flames."* After reading these verses I really wanted to know what kind of great loss the builder will suffer?

I know that when the time is right the Father will explain my question to me in a way that I will fully understand. I think in life at times we need patience and we need to wait for it, which is not always easy to do. Our Father truly loves the process of our growth in Him and if He would tell us everything at one time then what will we ever have to talk about the next time we meet together with Him. It is a good thing for each of us to be His work in progress! Because when the time arrives, we will be standing tall as all of our good works make their way through the fire and one by one, they will jump out of the fire, covering the ground and laying at our feet as countless jewels. I am going to pick up my jewels and give them to my Father.

Jesus The Pearl of Great Price

Our Father in heaven loves pearls, jewels, and gems and He loves to decorate with a lot of sparkle! He has extremely great taste. He loves bling and He is the greatest designer that ever was and is and is to come! Everything He designs is one of a kind. Here is a list of twelve gems He likes to stack on top of each other to create a splendid foundation. Revelation 21:19-21 *"The wall of the city was built on foundation stones inlaid with twelve gems: the first was jasper, the second sapphire, the third agate (chalcedony), the fourth emerald, the fifth onyx (sardonyx), the sixth carnelian (sardius), the seventh chrysolite, the eighth beryl, the ninth topaz, the tenth chrysoprase, the eleventh jacinth, the twelfth amethyst."* And in verse 21 this is what he likes to design using pearls: *"The twelve gates were made of pearls--- each gate from a single pearl! And the main street was pure gold, as clear as glass."* All who believe in His son Jesus will not perish but have everlasting life and we all will be living in a city of sparkle and bling! These scriptures are referring to the New Jerusalem on the New Earth when all the evil darkness is gone forever!

The current Heaven is pretty spectacular and it has a whole lot of sparkle and bling. It is huge and whenever I look at God's home from my window in my chamber, which is located in the atmosphere of the third heaven, God's home looks like a tremendous round planet. It is like a whole world in itself. I am sure other people who have taken a trip to visit heaven have seen many of the same things as I have seen.

I remember a day during the first week of March 2018. I had been asking God to increase my visits to heaven because I really like to travel. I see a lot of heaven when I am up and in my chamber, and there have been several times when Jesus has taken me right onto the planet called heaven. I do know the difference between when I am dreaming, having a vision, an open vision, seeing in the spirit, seeing something in my mind's eye, traveling in the spirit whether in the past, present, or the future, or when my whole physical body has been transported on the earth to another location, as I wrote about in my first book. I was visiting in Wisconsin and driving my rented car when the car, with me in it, was transported to a safer location. Since then it happened to me a second time here in North Carolina.

Like I said I love to travel! The Holy Spirit is currently teaching me that I can ask Him to take me traveling whenever I want. I do feel if I travel with him then it needs to have a purpose, a purpose where a new life will be brought into the kingdom or when someone needs healing and deliverance.

I often joke with my older sister, Penny, telling her not to freak out when one day she walks into her kitchen and I am standing there. I find the Holy Spirit likes holy fun. I am learning God's New ways of doing His work through me every day. He is teaching me that His Glory is available to consume me from the inside out. It is available for all of His beloved. I am an adventurous person and I want it all from God! I want everything He desires for me to have and to experience in Him. He is my everything! He became my Dad when I was lost and desperately in need of a Father. He showed up right on time and He has never left my side.

One thing I really enjoy is listening to the incredible heavenly singing. I often notice it happening as the sun begins to slowly rise up over the Blue Ridge Mountains. I am blessed to see this blue hue of color on these mountains but when I hear the singing, the blue color seems to be singing right along with the worship I hear floating down from the throne room. I still can recall the first morning I woke up hearing the singing.

I woke Jay up and he too could hear the singing. I also could hear an instrument playing which sounded like a piano and an organ all mixed into one instrument and it created an unusually beautiful sound. The sound seemed to create waves as if I could see the instrument itself. It looked like a wavy piano keyboard without legs floating in midair. I began to sing along with this new sound. This new sounding song repeated over and over again in two separate octaves, "Glo-ry, Glo-ry" as if the words were descending up and down in one graceful movement.

The second morning as the sun began to rise, I again heard the singing. It was a bit different because I could hear a male voice leading the worship. The third morning as I listened I felt I recognized the voice of the man and God said I recognized it correctly. It was the voice of a prophetic worship leader who was a very talented pianist who no longer lived on the earth but is now in heaven. His name was Kim Clement and he sounded amazing!

As the days passed, I continued to wake up to this singing until one morning I was woken up right before the sunrise was to begin. I was taken in my spirit by the Holy Spirit toward Heaven. I was very aware of what was happening. I began to hear the music as we drifted up to heaven and the closer we came to the world of heaven, the volume of the music intensified inside of me as if I had a front row seat to a concert. However, I did not see anything while we moved upwards. I realized God the Father was singing with them and I became undone. The Holiness of who He is penetrated my entire being from the sound of His voice. It deeply changed me. Rising up in me was a Holy fear and a tremendous respect for His Majesty, for who He is... He is God and there is NO other!

While I was listening in awe, the Holy Spirit took me to a place in Heaven as if He was giving me a private tour. Before me I saw the strangest white and glowing flying crafts. I realized there are crafts that are flown to pick up and transport a believer who has died from Earth to Heaven. As the Holy Spirit gave me a tour of this craft, I saw a man standing below us. He looked a bit blurry, but he was definitely there. I thought it was strange. I kept looking at all the intricate details on this craft. I was so fascinated! I didn't ask what this place was, so I decided to call this place a "transport station" because it housed these transports that were floating in the atmosphere of heaven. It reminds me of the star ships we see in movies like Star Wars, but these were so much better than anything man has ever designed.

When the visit was over, I immediately told Jay all the details and he had a quizzical look on his face, he said, "I think I traveled with you, but I was in a dream." I said, "You were the man I saw, that was you?" Jay said, "Next time I don't want to be stuck in the dream I want to be with you." I laughed and then told Jay I have been asking Father to allow us to go hand in hand while traveling around with the Holy Spirit. Jay agreed and smiled. We love to do things together. We make such a great team! *"Two people can accomplish more than twice as much as one; they get a better return for their labor."* Ecclesiastes 4:9

Twenty-Three

Gift Chamber

"God has given gifts to each of you from His great variety of spiritual gifts. Manage them well so that God's generosity can flow through you." 1 Peter 4:10.

A week or so after the golden portal had manifested on our deck I remember walking into our living room where I noticed Jay was spraying water on his favorite plant, a Peace Lily. This plant does not easily bloom but on this day two beautiful white flowers were in full bloom! Their scent filled our home with the aroma we often smell whenever Jesus is standing in our home. Jesus is scented with an aroma of Peace. *"And let the peace that comes from Christ rule in your hearts."* Colossians 3:15.

As Jay was tending his peace plant he noticed there were two sparkling specks of something unusual on one green leaf of his plant. I went to look and sure enough as I got a closer look there were two small shavings which looked like glistening green diamonds. These two specks were beautiful gifts that I wanted to capture so I took a video clip. To the date of this writing they are still glistening on Jay's plant. Two small gifts sent from a treasure house in heaven. This is the second time we received a shaving from a diamond, and I expect many more to be sent into our home for us to enjoy.

There are other believers in the body of Christ who have received gems and jewels from heaven as well as a substance that appears to look like gold dust. Some will see an oil that will glisten on people's skin, clothes or seep from objects. Jay and I often find gold glory glitter in our home. It will be glittering on our carpets, floors, or on objects. I often find it on the pages of my bible as I am reading. We also see this glory glitter sparkle on our clothes but when it appears on our skin it will glisten with rainbow colors. You can go on google and type in keywords and view some of these video clips these mysterious treasures from heaven but it's always a good idea to use the gift of discernment while viewing any of them.

I have a small box Tanique made for me when she was a little girl. In this box I store trinkets that Jesus sends to me from heaven. I like to write down on a note card the story that goes along with the gift and attach His gift to the card.

It is important to slow down during the day, to sit still, to listen and to look around because you never know when hidden things lingering around you will be exposed and become visible. Spiritual movement is alive, it is very active, and it is all around each one of us *every second of every day*. We never know when we will be standing smack dab in the middle of it until the Holy Spirit opens up our eyes to reveal His glory! Heaven is manifesting right now, wherever you are, and once you are able to experience it in your life you will never want it to stop! Ask God to pull back the veil on your eyes to see everything He has for you. God's love is so amazing! *"But blessed are your eyes, because they see; and your ears, because they hear."* Matthew 13:16.

Gifts

We are not to be ignorant regarding the spiritual gifts the Spirit of God has chosen to place inside each one of us? Each gift is to be used to build up the body of Christ. 1 Corinthians chapter 12 explains to us the different kinds of gifts that are given. I desire to be given every one of them! I have experienced many of these gifts. They flow out through me to build up His body. Often the gift of knowledge or prophecy will flow through me when I am ministering to a person.

It had been a few years into our marriage when I was helping Jay in his first accounting and tax business in Wisconsin. One of the duties I was in charge of was taking customers to the back office to hand them their finished tax returns if Jay was unavailable. I remember one instance where Jay had led an elderly gentleman to the back office by me and as soon as I saw him, I stood up from my chair to greet him with a handshake before Jay turned to leave the room. I will never forget what happened the moment I shook this gentleman's hand.

I instantly had the knowledge of the burden that he carried so heavily in his heart. I knew all the details of his ailing wife and I saw in my mind at that moment, his wife laying on the bed in their bedroom. I had the knowledge of this man's tremendous love for his wife and the worry that was consuming him. I felt overwhelmed at that time because it was the very first time this spiritual gift was used in this way by simply shaking his hand. When he left, I sat down in my chair to battle in the spirit on their behalf and the only way I knew to battle was to speak the words, "Help them Jesus." And then I felt peace.

"Blessed are the peacemakers, for they will be called sons of God." Matthew 5:9

"Each one should use whatever gift he has received to serve others, faithfully administering God's grace in its various forms." 1 Peter 4:10 (NIV)

Spiritual gifts are to be used for God's Glory because they are good! We need to remember that there are people who are ignorant to who Jesus is and often these people believe they have spiritual gifts and powers. They set up a businesses and go on various media outlets proclaiming to the world they can predict the future; calling themselves a psychic, medium, fortune teller, tarot card or palm reader to name a few.

Some people are steeped into witchcraft and they know the power was given to them from the devil. But some people do not know that because they dabble and really think they are helping people through their "gifting." Some even give God the credit but we know who is behind their witchcraft power. All spiritual gifts are God's creation. The devil can't create a single thing but he can copy what God has created to make it appear to be God's spiritual power. Many ignorant people have given the devil permission to manipulate them. I see it as a lack of knowledge and not God's gift of knowledge.

All of these people are easy ploys in the devil's hands. He will continue to lie and deceive them into thinking these false gifts are good and helpful. There are also people who use Christianity and mix it in with witchcraft practices. The gift of discernment is an essential gift to ask for because it is a gift any believer can use to discern between God's spirit and the spirit of the evil one. It is also used to test any demonic spiritual manifestation.

Remember, there are God's angels who show up as

well as evil angels and these evil angels are the ones who fell from Heaven with lucifer. 1 John 4:1 (NIV) declares, *"Dear Friends, do not believe every spirit, but Test the spirits to see whether they are gone out into the world."* I myself test angels or celestial beings who present themselves to me on the earth, in the spiritual realm, in visions and even in my dreams. I ask them, "Are you a spirit sent by the Spirit of the Most High God whose son is Jesus Christ who died on the cross for all mankind?" If they are evil angels / beings / spirits they will immediately leave or they may say something like, "It is as you say" or a similar vague statement. Sometimes I demand that they look at Jesus right now and to tell the truth. Then I know through their response, or lack of response, before I tell them to get out! But if they are sent from God they will answer with a yes and acknowledge the truth and God's presence fills the air.

With the gift of discernment, it is not hard to decide. There are believers who did not test the angel/being/spirit and they were taken to a false place, a false heaven or a false hell. We must be wise and test every encounter.

In the middle of summer 2019, I was in my bedroom, home alone, and I heard someone walking down our hallway towards our bedroom. I walked out our bedroom door and immediately I saw in the hallway a black shadow of a spirit which looked like a bent over crippled up old man. I spoke to test it while I was walking toward it and it quickly made an exit through our hallway wall and out of the house. I laughed and yelled at it saying, "And don't come back." It was funny. I then asked additional hosts to come into our home. Evil spirits, fallen angels, or celestial beings have no power in my home nor should they in yours! Me, my husband and even my daughter have had experiences with fallen angels who have bodies, but demons/evil spirits do not, they are bodiless but can manifest themselves.

There is no good witchcraft! Stay away from all forms! Sometimes psychics will hear the information right and sometimes they will not; or they are hearing nothing at all and just making it up as they go along. The enemy can create a false future through a psychic/medium. When someone asks a psychic about a dead loved one, or even a loved one who is alive, the enemy only knows information about the past or present.

Let me give you a personal example. There is a man who is a good friend of ours from Wisconsin. This man loves the lord and is gifted in his business and invented many new types of products. He came up with an idea and asked us, along with a few others, to help him with it and so we all did. This new idea was advertised on a local TV station and in interviews on two local popular radio stations. Everyone thought it was a great idea and proclaimed we were all going to make millions. Jay always believes God is our only provider and not man. So, as the very old saying goes "Don't count your chickens before they are hatched." and, "Don't write out checks your body can't cash."

Well, this man's wife who, was a religious woman, did something without *first* discussing it with her husband or Jesus. She decided to go to a local psychic to ask if this new idea would indeed make millions. It was funny because the psychic was told from the darkness to tell her that her husband would make a whole lot of money from this idea. The enemy is pretty sly and will lie about anything in order to capture and keep this woman far away from the lord. So the evil spirit told the psychic to tell her, "You will know I speak the truth because when your daughter comes home from school today and steps off the school bus she will see a dead squirrel lying on the ground." Guess what happened? Exactly, her daughter came running up their long driveway and stormed into the house extremely upset because right when she got off the school bus, she saw a yucky battered dead squirrel lying on the ground right next to her foot and she was horrified. Can you see how the enemy can present a false future and then seep a tormenting fearful spirit into this young girl's open heart from the shock of seeing this battered bloodied dead squirrel?

I remember after the man told us about this, I wanted to talk with his wife, but we never had the opportunity and this man never did make millions from the concept. The best thing I did was battle for his wife in the spiritual realm for God to wake her up and set her free by telling her the truth of whose power she was listening to. We choose with our own free will and our free will is powerful. Each person will choose to serve either the God of Heaven or the ruler of hell. It's a free choice, Heaven or hell, there is no in-between.

I have never heard a medium or psychic talk about a loved one who had died by telling the person that their loved one was in heaven and rejoicing around the throne of God. All the devil can come up with is they have crossed over, they are happy, or not to worry about them. The enemy cons people by encouraging them to stay involved in this occult activity in hopes he will get them to choose hell. By the way, the devil does know if the departed loved one is in heaven or hell and he sure is not going to spill the beans on either. We must keep interceding for all the people who are lost in darkness so they too will know the Lord and be set free. 1 Kings 8:60-61, *"May people all over the earth know that the Lord is God and that there is no other God. And may you, His people, always be faithful to the Lord our God. May you always obey His laws, and commands, just as you are doing today."*

Listen to the voice of God

"So why are you trying to find out the future by consulting mediums and psychics? Do not listen to their whisperings and mutterings. Can the living find out the future from the dead? Why not ask your God? Check their predictions against my testimony, says the Lord. "If their predictions are different from mine, it is because there is no light or truth in them." Isaiah 8:19-20.

You see, God's people were getting caught up in these occult practices because they were not listening to His voice or asking Him? Let us not follow in their examples. Always remember that we serve a God of forgiveness so ask for forgiveness and then ask God what to do next to get all darkness out of your heart.

I remember spending time with a young woman who tried but could not get close to Jesus. She always felt something was in the way. Her heart's desire was to be filled to overflowing with the giftings God had placed inside her but she felt they were somehow stuck. We joined hands together and asked Jesus what was the problem. Separately, we each asked Him as we sat together before Him.

It wasn't long after our prayers that she started to cry and began to tell me that before she was married, she went to see a psychic to ask if she would ever get married. She wanted a husband and children. She continued to cry and then started to sob. After she settled down a bit, she told me that the psychic told her she would have three children but her third child would die. This friend of mine was pregnant and into her second trimester with her third child. Well, that lie didn't go over well with me at all so together with Jesus, we broke this lie, this curse, and kicked that psychic spirit right out of her life and back to where it belonged. Months later my friend gave birth to a healthy beautiful baby boy! I guess God sure showed that evil psychic spirit who was boss!!!

Twenty-Four

Create Chamber

Why does satan copy? Because he can't create! I see satan trying to setup as many false religions as he can. He seems to try hard to corner the market on establishing as many false denominations as he can through people on earth. He takes a bit of truth and twists it with lies and it causes us to question how in the world could anyone fall for this. Unfortunately, many do. It has been going on for a very long time, but God always has a plan to do something about it! *"But forget all that----it is nothing compared to what I am going to do. For I am about to do a brand-new thing. See, I have already begun! Do you not see it?"* Isaiah 43:18-19. Whenever I read this verse, I respond to God's question by saying, "Yes, Yes Lord I do see it!" So what do I see? I see His glory. I see His invisible becoming visible all around me. I see His spirit covering the earth. I see His NEW!

I believe there are many brand-new things He is doing and will continue to do in the body of Christ. We must allow God to position us to be His light of newness to those around us. I do not want to be standing on the outside of this new Kingdom Age; I choose to be inside of it, fully submersed.

In 2013, Jay and I stood in our living room holding hands. We shouted out loud as we proclaimed to God, "We're jumping in." Then we literally jumped up, hand in hand, and over our imaginary line. We jumped into God's DNA, His Kingdom Age. It was awesome and I encourage you to jump in with us! The bible is full of strange actions which the Lord asked His people to do like we read in Ezekiel chapter four.

Ezekiel was asked to do quite a few strange things and one of them is found in verses 4 and 5. It says he was to lie on his left side for 390 days and then on his right side for 40 days. In the book of Hosea Chapter 1 verses 2 and 3 God told Hosea he was to marry a prostitute and it reads like this (NIV), *"The Lord began to speak through Hosea, the Lord said to him. "Go, take to yourself an adulterous wife and children of unfaithfulness, because the land is guilty of Diblaim, and she conceived and bore him a son."*

Jay and I have no problem jumping together over an imaginary line and into what God is doing on this earth. I am sure there are believers who feel the same but if you are not sure about all of this ask the Father. He will explain all things to you in a way you will understand. He knows each one of our personalities. He knows how we interpret things from Him, and He knows the best way to teach each one of us. What works for one may not work as well for another. *"My thoughts are completely different from yours," says the Lord. "And My Ways are far beyond anything you could imagine. For just as the heavens are higher than the earth, so are My Ways higher than Your Ways and My thoughts are higher than Your thoughts."* Isaiah 55:8-9.

For example, one person may feel led to pray in their heavenly language for one hour before they can go up to the heavens and into their chamber room. If that works for that person, great. But then another person may not need to do that, they may soar up by singing or listening to their favorite worship song. When I go up to heaven and into my chamber, I simply ask the Holy Spirit to take me up.

When someone declares you have to pray in the spirit for one hour or do this or that for any length of time, my advice would be to ask the Lord what is best for you. *"A person may think their own ways are right, but the Lord weighs the heart."* Proverbs 21:2 (NIV) If you feel you want to try to enter your chamber the way I or someone else does that's OK. It's also OK to ask the Lord to add to it so you and Jesus can make it your own special way of going up and into your very own chamber.

The same goes for fasting. I believe in fasting. I usually fast from food all morning and sometimes into mid-afternoon. I like to fast all the while I am in my chamber. This is something the Lord stirred in my heart and has been my life since 2011. But please remember, someone may have great results from a certain length of fasting and God may want you to do the same but He may want you to change it up and do something different. You have to ask Him what He wants for you. The Lord has plans for each one of us and He may want to prepare us through fasting first before moving forward in any of His plans.

I continue to watch many believers become too co-dependent on what pastors, prophets, leaders, mentors, or other believers tell them to do. I believe these people can actually come in-between a believer and God. It's like they are the mediator to Jesus. Jesus is our only mediator between us and God, not any person. Scripture tells us how important it is to ask for increased discernment. I like to ask daily for it and throughout the day whenever I need extra help. Discernment comes from the spirit. It is an awesome gift. Sound wisdom comes from the Father in heaven. *"If you need wisdom---if you want to know what God wants you to do---ask Him, and He will gladly tell you. He will* not resent your asking." James 1:5. Discernment can be given in a second. *"For wisdom will enter your heart, and knowledge will fill you with joy. Wise planning will watch over you. Understanding will keep you safe."* Proverbs 2:10-11. God will direct us and His wise plans will keep us riding on the waves of His Glory without ever falling off. *"Now unto Him that is able to keep you from falling, and to present you faultless before the presence of His glory with exceeding joy."* Jude 1:24 (KJB)

Every day in our home we have angel and glory activity. Jay and I see them both on a regular basis. In fact, as I am typing this chapter on my laptop, I am sitting on a comfortable stool at my bistro table in my kitchen. All day today, I have been very aware of white robed angels moving about inside of our home. I saw a side view of a glistening white robe as it passed to the left of me. We are very comfortable with their presence in our home and following us around wherever we go. Jay and I have noticed that as each of us continue to go up and into our chambers to be with Jesus, not only does our intimacy with Him increase but also the number of angels and glory activity we see everyday is also increasing.

"For He will command His angels concerning you to guard you in all your ways." Psalm 91:11 (NIV)

I encourage you to stop a moment and ask God if He

would bring back to your memory some of the times He sent His angels to guard you in all your ways. I know when we go home to heaven we will be able to watch a movie of our lives from before birth to the day we arrive in Heaven. We will view all the events of "guarding" that happened in our lifetime on the earth. I know I will be amazed at the countless times God guarded me.

"He had a dream, and behold, a ladder was set on the earth with its top reaching to heaven; and behold, the angels of God were ascending and descending it." Genesis 28:12 (NASB). God is bringing back to my memory a time when His angels gave me protection.

I finished my grocery shopping and I was placing my few bags of groceries in the back seat of my car. My body was half in and half out of the car. The door of the car was half closed and it was pressing on the side of my body. I remember turning my head as I felt a car was turning to park in the stall next to me. I saw there was not enough room for the woman who was driving to properly park with my door still half open. It was obvious to me that she was not slowing down enough to safely enter the parking space. I felt she didn't care that my car door was blocking her way. In the spirit, I knew in that instant that the enemy had a plan and was trying to use this woman's careless and inattentive driving to seriously hurt me. I also remember a man was walking towards me to his parked car which was on the other side of my car. All I could say out loud was NO!

I blinked my eyes and when I opened them I saw the woman confused and wondering how she got into the parking stall right next to my car. I closed my car door while the woman sat there dazed. I looked over the roof of my car and I saw the man now standing by the passenger door of his car to place his grocery bags inside. His face looked upset as he looked directly at me and asked if I was alright because he had seen the woman was headed right for me. I quickly said, "Yes, Jesus protected me," and the man nodded his head.

God definitely protected me from being crushed by my car door. I praised Him all the way home for His angel protection! But the best part is... I never felt angry at this woman. All I could think about doing was to ask Father God to make sure she will be with me in Heaven and to help her stay alert anytime she is driving or parking her car.

Anointing Power

This is a battle phrase I proclaim throughout my day. *"I release the anointing Power of God's Glory through me to clear away all darkness!"* I also speak these words out loud over my husband, my children, their spouses and all of my grandchildren. It Works!!! God created words. His words, like His angels, are a guarding wall of protection all around us. *"The Lord keeps you from all evil and preserves your life. The Lord keeps watch over you as you come and go, both now and forever."* Psalm 121:7-8. I am so blessed that these scripture verses were written to be spoken to preserve me from evil as I come and go, especially when I am doing my grocery shopping! Thank You Jesus!

Twenty-Five

Step Chamber

"How can we understand the road we travel? It is the Lord who directs our Steps." This verse is found in Proverbs 20:24 and it is a verse I meditate on because I want to understand. It is important for me to understand. Jay and I have taken countless steps before the understanding comes. Sometimes it's hard but we do it anyway. We have traveled way beyond taking baby steps. Our steps today are more like leaps. Each individual leap lands us safely onto a new step. As we continue to mature in Christ our gift of faith increases. This increased faith then allows us to leap even higher onto so many more new steps. Our faith is lifting us up higher. We will not fall because the angels help us to succeed, and that is one thing I do understand. *"Hold up my goings in thy paths, that my footsteps slip not."* Psalm 17:5 (KJB) We will not slip, we will not fall off the steps we leap to as long as we follow

His path, even when we do not understand. Lord, I will obey you! *"Mark out a straight path for your feet; then stick to the path and stay safe. Don't get sidetracked; keep your feet from following evil."* Proverbs 4:26-27.

What path are you on? If a believer gets sidetracked can the believer get back on the straight path? The Holy Spirit led me to read in chapter three of Lamentations verses 23, 24, 31, 32 & 33 which say, *"Great is His faithfulness; His mercies begin afresh each day. I say to myself, The Lord is my inheritance; therefore, I will hope in Him! ... For the Lord does not abandon anyone forever. Though He brings grief, He also shows compassion according to the greatness of His unfailing love. For He does not enjoy hurting people or causing them sorrow."* When I read these scripture verses, I am not concerned when it says, "He brings grief," because I love to obey Him.

When we feel fearful in our steps it's probably because we know we have not obeyed Him fully. But He is the God of love and compassion and His love has a way of steering us back into His straight path of protection. If we refuse to obey and purposefully go off the path to take a shortcut, He will make it known to us that He is not pleased. If we refuse to listen, God has no problem putting one of His children on the time out chair.

In 2015 I remember the Lord led me to watch a

famous prophetic minister whose reputation provided Him with respect in the body of Christ. Unfortunately, this man had at times a short fuse. As I was listening to this man worship God, He paused and then began to speak words from the Father in heaven. He stopped while he was giving the words and asked for one of his team members to hand him an object to represent what was being said. When the object was not handed to him quickly enough, he condescendingly chastised his team members right on the live-stream.

I was a bit startled, not at what he did but at the words Father shared with me, "He is going on a time-out chair." I had no idea what that meant but what ended up happening was that a few weeks later the man ended up in the hospital with his body in a paralyzed state for a length of time. Then God took him home. I asked God, "Why?" He shared with me that He did not want this man to jeopardize his salvation because of the anger issues he would not control. I remember listening to one of his family members saying humorously that one time he became angry and threw a piece of equipment he was using off his desk. I believe God is so compassionate that he can take anyone of his children home if they are in a place where He knows it is better for them to leave than to stay. Isaiah 57:1-2 gives us additional insight as it says, *"The righteous pass away, the godly often die before their time. And no one seems to care or wonder why. No one seems to understand that God is protecting them from the evil to come. For the godly who die will rest in peace."*

We serve a mysterious God and indeed His thoughts and His ways are surely not our thoughts or our ways. I have a great reverence for my Father in heaven as His eternal wisdom cannot even begin to fit inside of my mind. But His eternal love can fill my heart to know my God is in complete control. I am safe! I have His promises in my heart. We serve a God of promises. He is a God who keeps His promises! *"Now I am about to go the way of all the earth. You know with all your heart and soul that not one of all the good promises the Lord your God gave you failed. Every promise has been fulfilled; not one has failed.* Joshua 23:14 (NIV)

Not only do we serve a God who can take us home when He decides but He also is a God who can bring us back from the dead. And He can even add years to our life as we read in Isaiah 38:4-6 *"Then this message came to Isaiah from the Lord: "Go back to Hezekiah and tell him, 'This is what the Lord, the God of your ancestor David, says: I have heard your prayer and seen your tears. I will add fifteen years to your life, and I will rescue you and this city from the king of Assyria. Yes, I will defend this city."* He is a God who gives people specific instructions just like He did with Moses before he went home to heaven. Deuteronomy 32:49-50. *"Go to Moab, to the mountain east of the river, and climb Mount Nebo, which is across from Jericho. Look out across the land of Canaan, the land I am giving to the people of Israel as their own possession. Then you must die there on the mountain and join your ancestors, just as Aaron, your brother, died on Mount Hor and joined his ancestors."*

Come Home

In early winter 2018 I had gone to bed for the night and I was about to fall asleep. I was alerted to a severe pain in my heart and I knew my heart was going to stop beating. I was not afraid because I knew I would go home to be with my Father. While I felt the pain, I saw a structure in the spirit and at the same time heard Jesus tell me that the last section of my mansion was complete. He then asked me a question. He said, "Would you like to come home now?" I remember telling Him, "No, I want to stay and continue. Just add another wing on to my mansion and when that one is complete keep adding on wings." After I answered Jesus, I realized the severe pain in my heart stopped and I fell asleep.

This was the second time I had a severe pain in my heart. The first time was during the first year we came to live in North Carolina in 2011. It was later in the evening. I remember I was sitting on our sofa when I felt an extreme pain pierce my heart and quickly the entire left side of my body went numb. I remember speaking out loud as I commanded this pain and numbness to leave in Jesus name and immediately it left. That was a demonic attack but the other pain I felt while lying in bed in 2018 was not.

One thing I am certain of is that Jesus paid the price for me on the cross and He took the keys of death away from satan! I like the bible verse in 1 Corinthians 15:54-55 *"Death is swallowed up in victory. O death, where is your victory? O death, where is your sting?"* 2 Kings chapter 2 tells us about when God sent a whirlwind to take the prophet Elijah up and away. He never died and was never buried. In Hebrews chapter 7 we read about someone named Melchizedek who was the king of Salem and a priest of God. In verse three it says, *"There is no record of his father or mother or any of his ancestors---no beginning or end to his life. He remains a priest forever, resembling the Son of God."* This one, sent from heaven, had no records of his birth on this earth, no death, and no burial either.

I pray every day and declare for myself, Jay, our children and their families that none of us will die but rather be taken up to be with Him. It doesn't necessarily have to be when Jesus will *unexpectedly* come to take out His entire bride from the earth. We as a family still have a lot of work to do with the Lord to fulfill our purposes on this earth, as individuals and together, because we are His bridal tribe. I believe we can live a long time on this earth maybe even hundreds of years.

It's all up to the Father and what He has decided.

There is something about death being swallowed up. Nothing is impossible! He is a God who does new things! The Holy Word of God contains new revelations that are coming alive to me every day. Sometimes my understanding of them may be hidden for a time but now they are springing forth! I believe FAITH has everything to do with the impossible becoming possible.

Faith creates Miracles! Can my family be taken up without ever dying? I believe YES we can! *"It was by faith that Enoch was taken up to heaven without dying---"suddenly he disappeared because God took him." But before he was taken up, he was approved as pleasing to God. "So, you see, it is impossible to please God without faith. Anyone who wants to come to Him must believe that there is a God and that He rewards those who sincerely seek Him."* Hebrews 11:5-6. I love to sincerely seek Him, my God. I know He loves you and I know He is calling His children to "Come On Up!" He is waiting to take you up and into your own chamber in heaven so He can reveal Himself to you and increase in you His abundant life!

"The Spirit and the bride say, "Come." Let each one who hears them say, "Come." Let the thirsty ones come---anyone who wants to. Let them come and drink the water of life without charge." Revelation 22:17

Twenty-Six

Tribe Chamber

Genesis 35:23-26 lists the names of the twelve sons of Jacob. In Genesis 32:28 God changed Jacob's name to be called Israel. The names of the twelve sons of Jacob/Israel are the following: Reuben, Simeon, Levi, Judah, Dan, Naphtali, Gad, Asher, Issachar, Zebulun, Joseph and Benjamin. In genesis chapter 49 Jacob blessed his twelve sons before he died and what he said would happen to each one of them in the days to come did happen. Some of the blessings were good and some not so good. The blessings seemed to mirror who they were and how they lived and served their God. It was from these twelve sons of Jacob that the Twelve Tribes of Israel were named and established.

After Moses died God spoke to Joshua, son of Nun, who was Moses' assistant and gave him the strategies to lead God's Tribes across the Jordan River and into the land He promised. You can read all the details of this take over in the book of Joshua. The Twelve Tribes of Israel took dominion over the lands of the North, South, East and West to dwell in according to God's promises.

The Northern Tribes:

Dan, Asher, and Naphtali

The Southern Tribes:

Reuben, Simeon, and Gad

The Eastern Tribes:

Judah, Issachar, and Zebulun

The Western Tribes:

Ephraim, Manasseh, and Benjamin

Levi is not listed as one of the twelve tribes of Israel here because no Land was given to the descendants of Levi as we read in Joshua 13:14 *"Moses did not assign any land to the tribe of Levi. Instead, as the Lord had promised them, their offerings burned on the altar to the Lord, the God of Israel."* There were men who were chosen by God to be priests within the tribe of Levi. All Israelites who belonged to the tribe of Levi received this inheritance. *"Remember that the Levitical priests and the rest of the tribe of Levi will Not be given an inheritance of land like the other tribes in Israel. Instead, the priests and Levites will eat from the offerings given to the Lord by fire, for that is their inheritance. They will have no inheritance of their own among the Israelites. The Lord himself is their inheritance, just as He promised them."* Deuteronomy 18:1-2.

Another fact I found interesting was that Joseph's name was also not listed as a tribe of Israel. Instead, his tribe was so extensive that his tribe split into two tribes bearing the names of his twin sons, Manasseh and Ephraim. His Egyptian wife Asenath bore the sons to Joseph while he was a captive in Egypt.

A definition of the word Tribe is, "Any aggregate of people united by ties of descent from a common ancestor, community of customs and traditions, adherence to the same leaders."

In 2004 Jesus stirred my heart to research my heritage on my mother's side and then later on my father's side. It became a fun project for Jay, Tanique and I. We found many records on my mother's side with the help of the Lord, we began to track down and unlock a family secret. A secret that had been protected for many years with promises to never disclose our family's Native American heritage. My great-great grandmother, who was a full-blooded Indian, decided to hide her Indian heritage through marriage to my great-great grandfather who was of German descent. My great-grandmother and my grandmother also married men who were of strong German descent.

On my father's side of the family my grandparents

were both one hundred percent Swedish and we even found my grandfather's signature in one of the books at Ellis Island in New York where he arrived by ship from Gothenburg, Sweden.

So, one half of my DNA makeup is Swedish and the other half is Indian and German. Myself, my mother, my first son Ian, my second brother Monte, and a few of my cousins have strong Indian resemblances from our American Indian heritage. I am thankful for the day when Jesus stirred in my heart to research the importance of belonging to a tribe. We were researching for a long time to find the name of my Indian tribe and one day Jesus stepped in.

I remember the day as if it were yesterday. We were living in Wisconsin and pastoring Cornerstone Youth Church. I went to a city festival being held in the park behind our ministry building. It was a Saturday. I was standing in the middle of the park with all the activity going on around me. I noticed a man and a woman getting off a festival trolley tour bus. I watched them turn to their left and then they both began walking toward me. It felt as if they appeared out of the blue! When they reached me, the woman started talking to me as if she knew me personally, as if I were a part of them. This was indeed a divine encounter! Time seemed to slow down and the activity around me faded away.

After the woman greeted me, she began to tell

me that she was a full-blooded Apache Indian. Her husband was also Native American and was from the Lakota tribe. He showed me a red birthmark located on one of his thumbs and told me that males from his tribe are born with it. The woman from the Apache tribe took my hand and placed my fingers at the base of her neck slightly below her head and as she moved my fingers up and down I felt there was a definite bump. She told me that all Apaches have this bump.

I began explaining to both of them the research we had embarked on in trying to locate my grandmother's tribe. I continued to tell them how important it was for me to find our tribe as it had been kept a secret for many years. Both of them listened intently and after I finished the woman said, "I know your tribe. You are Blackfoot. You have the distinct long face and the long bridge on your nose."

When she told me this my spirit leapt inside me and I knew we were closer to solving the secret. This woman also wrote down on a piece of paper for me the name of an Indian woman who was gifted in helping people locate their Indian tribe.

Jay and I did more research that evening on the internet. We found and printed out a picture of a Blackfoot Indian woman and when we looked at it, we realized it looked just like me! I felt like I was looking at my twin. I have seen pictures of my mother when she was a girl and she too looked like a Blackfoot Indian.

My mother has seen a picture of one of her grandmothers in her Indian wardrobe. I have talked to my second cousin and she told me that she will try to find the picture of our grandmother. She inherited all the old pictures when her mother passed away who was a sister to my grandmother. My cousin went on to tell me that her mother promised to keep the information a secret so the truth behind our Indian heritage would never be exposed. My cousin's only brother also knew all the details. He too was entrusted by their mother with the secret and has passed away keeping that secret.

My second cousin vaguely remembers overhearing several conversations between her mother, her brother and my great-grandmother while growing up in their home on the farm. I imagine them discussing the stories of life as an Indian when my great-grandmother was a girl. My cousin said she wishes she would have listened more intently during her childhood.

My God has a way of unlocking any secret because He knows everything! All we have to do is ask Him for help and the fun journey will begin. It's a fun scavenger hunt, one clue leads to another clue until the prize is found. God created the Indian heritage and it is a heritage I am blessed to have.

As I continued to research with the Lord, I learned

that my tribe is indeed Blackfoot but it is the Blackfoot/ Sioux tribe. The Blackfoot/Sioux Tribe, also known as the Sihasapa are a division of the Lakota tribe who came into Wisconsin from Minnesota because the tribe was continually being pushed out of their homeland in North and South Dakota.

In August of 2020 Jay and I drove to Fond du Lac, Wisconsin to attend my son's wedding. A couple of days after the wedding we decided to drive to Woodbury, Minnesota to visit my oldest son. At one point in western Wisconsin, I distinctly heard God's voice say to me, "Look over to your right" and when I turned my head I had a clear vision from the Lord. I saw a plain with trees and a river flowing nearby. I saw a large group of Indian men, women, and children of all ages. I saw elderly men and women, young adults and children. I saw babies in papooses being carried on their mother's back. I saw the chief, the warriors, and the medicine man. I saw the Teepee's they lived in and all the busy activity of their daily lives from cooking their food on top of the fires, tanning hides, riding horses, hunting, fishing, dancing, playing games. I saw all the activities of the everyday life of the American Indian.

I then heard God say, "Your tribe lived here." God allowed me to view the life of my past ancestors from my Blackfoot/Sioux Indian Tribe.

When the vision ended God immediately directed

me to a road sign that said Black River. I then saw a sparkling, flowing river and it was a special feeling to know this was the same river I had just seen in my vision. My tribe lived on this plain which was close to the Black River and near the Minnesota state line while they lived in Wisconsin. This is so fascinating because we had done research in a few counties in Wisconsin and have found three generations of my Indian grandmothers on my mother's bloodline. We were able to find their birth, marriage, death certificates and other information. Wisconsin has a rich history of Indian tribes who settled throughout Wisconsin to live. Many artifacts have been found and books have been written about each tribe and their history. There are also small Indian museums in many of the counties in Wisconsin.

After the Lord revealed to me who my Indian Tribe was, it explained why I have such a tremendous determination to be a Bridal Warrior for Christ, wanting to defeat the enemy of darkness. I had learned that this Blackfoot/Sioux tribe were fierce warriors and deeply spiritual and it was the famous Sitting Bull who led and united the Sioux people in their struggle for survival on the north American plains.

When I was in my early twenties my mother was so determined to take a vacation along with my dad and my youngest brother to North and South Dakota.

Now I know why, it is the land of her Blackfoot/Sioux Indian Tribe. Even though she wasn't aware of it at the time, I know the Lord drew her back to visit the roots of her true tribal land. I pray that all the Tribes of all the Nations will know the Lord and accept Him into their lives as the one true Spirit, their Creator God!

It reminds me of what is still happening to this day in Israel as God declared in His Holy Word that He would bring back His people to their homeland. They were once scattered all throughout the nations and now, one by one, they are being drawn back home to the land of their ancestors. Ezekiel 11:17, *"I, the Sovereign Lord, will gather you back from the nations where you are scattered, and I will give you the land of Israel once again."*

I asked God exactly when in history did my Indian heritage begin and He told me it was at the Tower of Babel. It was when He came down and gave the people different languages which caused the people to scatter (see Genesis Chapter 11). The Lord also revealed to me in the winter of 2018 two of the land areas the people of my Indian heritage scattered to live in after God halted the building of the Tower of Babel and gave the people different languages. The land areas were called India and Malaysia. He continued to show me Indians in a group walking as they crossed over a land bridge and came into North America.

In 2017 Father revealed to me which of the twelve tribes of Israel my husband and I are connected with. I am connected with the tribe of Naphtali and my husband is connected with the tribe of Asher through our mothers' sides. My father's mother is connected to the tribe of Zebulun. Jay's father's mother is connected to the tribe of Gad. It was even more interesting when Jay's mother informed us that she had her DNA tested and it contains 8% European Jew. It has been and continues to be an amazing journey of research especially in knowing more of the history about the tribe of Naphtali and the tribe of Asher. It reveals to me so much of who we are in Him.

Our God is full of information and He loves to reveal to us more of who we are in Him and who we are in our ancestral genealogy. All of us began with the same DNA of our Father in Heaven. If I stop to think about it, we are all connected. *"After this I saw a vast crowd, too great to count, from every nation and tribe and people and language, standing in front of the throne and before the Lamb. They were clothed in white and had palm branches in their hands."* Revelation 7:9. In Isaiah 54:5 it says, *"For your Creator will be your husband, The Lord Almighty is His name!"*

We, the body of Christ, male and female, we who have accepted the lamb, belong to Him. We are to be His pure and spotless brides on this earth! We are a tribe, a tribe of brides! We are called to operate as a remnant Bride of Christ! The bible speaks of tribes and nations. There are twelve tribes of Israel. The angels too were created in tribes. The word tribe is so interesting to me.

When Jesus led us here to North Carolina to live in our Promised Land, to take dominion, and to rule as His brides; He began to call us, our children and their families, a Bridal Tribe. He chose Jay and I to live the life of remnant warrior brides. He has set us up to lead, to teach, to encourage His body of believers to rise up, to be His brides, to go and take spiritual dominion and to rule in their own promised lands. The bride is able to speak out and release God's tribe of Host angels in Jesus name to kick out all the darkness of the enemy and take over their lands of promise! Our promised lands are a reward for our good work as the Lord revealed to me in Ezekiel 29:20 *"Yes, I have given him the land of Egypt as a reward for his work, says the Sovereign Lord, because he was working for me when he destroyed Tyre."*

Jay and I have been hidden, but now it is our time to shine! A very tall order, but for us the taller the better! We have been prepared, we have been tested, tried and true. We spend countless hours in our bridal chambers. We are living in our land of promise as the bride of Christ. We are living the life of Chamber Brides moving in His supernatural power right here in North

Carolina. We are working the land. Our Father will determine our coming and our going as we also will fly all over this earth. We Are Ready to Soar!!!!! Ok, Yes, I am excited!

I love the plan the Father has purposed for us, His brides in His body, His congregation! He died for us and He has come to break man's religious church system apart inside the heart, soul and mind of the believer so when His people gather together with two or more, the Holy Spirit will have one hundred percent control of the meeting regardless the size. His way not our way! This is how Jay and I are being the remnant bride wherever we are! We will not be locked up in a religious church system. We have been set free to live in freedom!

This breaking is happening on the earth and it will continue to happen as the Brides of Christ choose to rise up, to live in His glory power every second of every day as His signs and wonders freely flow out through each one of us. Father, I choose you to control my life, I trust You!!

I encourage you to spend time up and in your own Bridal Chamber talking with our Jesus, our groom. Our beloved will lovingly fill you and move through you to live the life of His bride. We welcome you into the tribe, His bridal tribe!

Twenty-Seven

Sky Chamber

At the end of June 2013, Jay, myself and Tanique were in Wisconsin to meet our second granddaughter and to bring my nephew, Shane, back to North Carolina with us for a visit. I love flying in God's beautiful sky. We were having a nice time in the jet talking about the Lord. But as we came closer to the Blue Ridge mountains, the weather turned into a turbulent rain storm. Our mid-size jet began rocking and shaking. A man who was sitting in the seat behind Shane started to have an emotional melt down and was becoming terrified.

Tanique and I were sitting across the aisle from Jay and Shane. Tanique and I started to silently pray for this man. The four of us were not afraid, it just felt like a roller coaster ride and we knew Jesus was controlling the ride. It was so fun to watch the Holy Spirit prompt Shane to be the one who was to minister to this man.

Shane turned in his seat and raised himself up far enough so the man could see his face and look into his eyes.

Shane began to explain to him how everything would be ok because of Jesus. The tender love and compassion we heard in his voice was spoken with confidence and strength. As the words flowed through Shane, they were breaking the fear, they were calming this man. Shane told the man not to worry, he knew from Jesus that it was not his time to die. Shane reassured him with genuine love in his voice that the plane would continue to fly and we would safely land at the Asheville airport. The rain storm continued outside of the jet but inside the jet the storm was subsiding. That was a great flight home! We landed peacefully.

Like I said I love to fly and our bridal tribe has a great love for aviation. We all love to fly and travel. We have four adult children. Our second son and our daughter-in-law have soared in aviation as pilots and flight instructors. Our daughter-in-law, by the grace of God has fulfilled her dream as she pilots an F-16 fighter jet. Our first son, who is married to this F-16 pilot, excels as an air traffic controller. He has received many recognitions in his career and he knows how to fly a plane. We also have our third son who will be pursuing a private pilot license in the near future as well as Jay.

All the rest of our children, their spouses and our grandchildren also enjoy flying. The Lord keeps revealing to me that we will be spending more time in the air than on the ground and that is just fine with me! Psalms 37:4-5 *"Take delight in the Lord, and He will give you your heart's desires."* And *"Commit everything you do to the Lord. Trust Him and He will help you."* My family and I have seen these two verses come to life in our lives over and over.

All of our children and their spouses are blessed with incredible gifts and talents. God has led us and taught us as parents how to raise our children up in their God given gifts and talents to be men and women of God in the marketplace. It first began at home with us nurturing their relationships with Jesus throughout their childhood as their gifts were discovered before they pursued their careers to live their adult lives. *"Train up a child in the way he should go, and when he is old he will not depart from it."* Proverbs 22:6 (RSV)

Let's Go Fishing

Romans 1:20-23 *"From the time the world was created, people have seen the earth and sky and all that God made. They can clearly see His invisible qualities--His eternal power and divine nature. So they have no excuse whatsoever for not knowing God.*

Yes, they knew God, but they wouldn't worship Him as God or even give Him thanks. And they began to think up foolish ideas of what God was like. The result was that their minds became dark and confused. Claiming to be wise, they became dark and confused. Claiming to be wise, they became utter fools instead.

And instead of worshiping the glorious, ever-living God, they worshiped idols made to look like mere people, or birds and animals and snakes."

We had a good time while my nephew was with us after landing in Asheville from that exciting flight and we kept getting into "Good God Trouble." On one beautiful sunny afternoon Tanique and I decided to take Shane to a popular waterfall called Hooker Falls. We decided to pack a lunch and grab our comfortable lawn chairs while Shane packed up his fishing gear. When we arrived at the falls it was quiet. There were only a few people enjoying the falls and after a short time those few people left and we had the place all to ourselves. It felt so good sitting in the warm sun while viewing God's tremendous beauty and listening to the sound of the water rushing over the falls. It was peaceful.

Shane picked a spot to fish but after a while it was obvious nothing was biting. I looked up at the sky and noticed one large rain cloud had drifted in and hovered directly over us. It was strange that this beautiful sunny cloudless day quickly produced a large rain cloud. I felt the spiritual atmosphere change, so I stood up from my lawn chair and decided to walk to a large rock and stand on it. The rock was a short distance from where Shane had moved to in hopes of finding a spot where he would catch a fish.

I stood watching Shane throw out his line and reel it back in. I looked off to my left and I noticed a middle-aged woman sitting on a large rock. She was definitely of Native American heritage. I could tell that she too was enjoying the serenity of the falls and the smallness of the crowd. A few seconds later it started to sprinkle and as I looked up at the cloud the sprinkles were quickly turning into a rain shower. I immediately spoke out loud as I lifted my arms up in the air. I thanked God for making the rain cloud and for sending the rain, but I also wanted it to stop raining so we could stay longer for Shane to catch a fish. I took authority over the weather and, said "In Jesus' name I command the rain cloud to stop flowing so Shane can catch a fish."

As I was speaking out loud, I remember Shane began to laugh and at the same time the Indian woman came over and stood by me to join in with me because she thought I was giving praise to the spirit living in the rain cloud. Indians so often believe there is a sprit living in animals or in the creation of nature and so on. The Indian woman stood by me looking up at the cloud. She joined in with me by lifting up her arms to the unknown spirit living in the cloud. But instead of praising an unknown spirit she heard me praising the one true God who made the cloud and in the name of His son Jesus she heard His power speak to the cloud to stop raining and to her amazement the rain immediately stopped!

At that moment two things happened. The rain stopped and Shane reeled in a beautiful speckled Trout! He was excited! He told us this was a first for him. He had never caught a speckled trout before. God decided to pour out His brand-new experiences for Shane and for this Indian woman. All of us were excited. It was God's "New" that opened up a window of opportunity.

As the Indian woman and I were standing there on that rock with a dark rain cloud over us, I was able to tell this woman who God is and how much He loved her. I told her what the blood of Jesus, God's son, did for her on the cross and how incredible it is to be filled with His Holy Spirit. Her eyes saw the glory power of the three in one. The heavens opened up on the earth and all God did was send one dark rain cloud in the sky above us. It rained and opened up her sky so I could share with her how to accept His son Jesus into her heart, to receive the one true God who has the power to stop the rain cloud from raining.

Immediately after I shared this with her, I asked if she wanted to accept the Lord Jesus into her heart and she simply nodded her head yes. No words were spoken, only this one motion of **Yes** set things in motion for her to receive Jesus and she became brand new. Heaven went fishing and caught itself a fish! I really like the whole fishing analogy God arranged. The Holy Spirit asked me to give her a copy of my first book which I had a copy of in my backpack. I gave her the copy and she gladly received it and with a big smile on her face she walked away.

After Shane took his new fish off the hook, he returned it to the water and we decided to leave. We packed up our belongings and began our ten-minute walk back down the mountain trail which led to the parking lot. I remember as we were slowly driving out of the parking lot the Holy Spirit had me turn my head to look out the back window of our car and I saw the Indian woman. She was walking out from among the thick row of trees which led to several other water falls. I saw that while she was walking to her car, she was intently reading my book.

I noticed that when she reached her car she sat down on a tree stump and seemed to be devouring the words in my book which contain life giving scripture verses. I knew God's words and all the experiences he has given me to write about in this book would help bring her into a new way of living a powerful life in Christ. Her first bridal experience happened that day. She's HOOKED! *"Come, follow me, "Jesus said, "and I will send you out to fish for people."* Matthew 4:19

(NIV) The Holy Spirit revealed to me that she would be sharing this New experience with all of her tribe. The woman didn't tell me who her tribe was but I discerned it was Cherokee. Wow! Now that was some really great God trouble we all got into. That day began as a day full of sunshine but turned into a shower. It rained in new life and washed a sinner clean!

"Purify me from my sins, and I will be clean; wash me, and I will be whiter than snow." Psalm 51:7

Twenty-Eight

Bridal Chamber

Live the life of a Chamber Bride

How can we prepare ourselves to be a pure and spotless Bride without wrinkle? I felt led by the Holy Spirit to ask Jay to share with us his discernment and thoughts.

In 2019 someone shared a short video on Facebook by a younger, prominent, up and coming pastor of a large church whose main campus is not far from where we live here in Western North Carolina. This is a pastor of a church that has a number of "satellite" churches around the area and maybe even beyond this region. He is becoming well known on the internet as well.

I want to quote word for word to you what the pastor said in the video clip. As you read this, know up front what he says is absolutely false. Jamie has struggled with how disjointed this quote is and has tried to change it to make it more understandable, but I have had to change it back to exactly what he said. Yes, it is completely confusing and extremely difficult to understand but it is part of what I need you to understand as I move on to describe living as a bride. So here is the quote;

"I've been reading in John 15 every day and what he said. I've tried to find in John 15 where Jesus said 'Maintain your love for me.' I can't find it. All I can find is Matthew 26 where He says, "You'll all fall away.' Every single one of you are going to go through seasons where you lose sight of your calling. Every single one of you are going to go through seasons where your character is all over the place. Every single one of you are going to go through seasons where you lose your connection to other people. But Jesus didn't say maintain your love for me. And that's how we live. 'Oh man, I just gotta love God more. I gotta love Jesus more. I gotta love Him more. I gotta love Him more. But He never said, 'Maintain your love for me.' He said, 'Remain in my love for you.' What's the secret of sustainable success? It's not your ability to maintain your love for Jesus. It's your willingness to remain in His love for you."

He couldn't be more wrong!!!!! And I say it again, **He couldn't be more wrong!!!!!** As I mentioned, what he said is utter confusion, lies and deception. Is there any wonder that all those listening to him and agreeing with him are living a life where there are seasons where they lose sight of their calling, seasons where their character is all over the place? He completely missed the greatest commandment where Jesus tells us in Matthew 22 verses 35 through 37, *"And one of them, a lawyer, asked Him a question to test Him. 'Teacher, which is the great commandment in the law?' And He said to him, 'You shall love the Lord your God with all your heart and with all your soul and with all your mind."* (ESV) Jesus says the greatest commandment is to love the Lord your God, **NOT** remain in His love. I realized the 4th time through editing this book that God gave Jamie this same verse and lesson in chapter nine - Love Chapter.

I pray for this pastor because God will take him off his high and mighty throne. He will come down and unless he repents and turns from his prideful ways *"It would be better for him if a millstone where hung around his neck and he were cast into the sea than that he should cause one of these little ones to sin."* Luke 17:2 (ESV) I wanted to share that sermon snippet because loving God is integral to being a Bride of Christ. You can **NOT** be a bride of Christ without loving Him with every part of your heart, mind and soul.

When you think about a bride, what is the first thing

that you picture in your mind? What is it that she talks about the most? Who does she desire to spend the most time with in her life? In today's world, whose picture is constantly showing up on her social media page and as the screen saver on her smart phone? Who will she leave all her friends hanging to go be with?

When I picture a bride, I see someone who is consumed with love for her groom. When she looks at him, everything else in the world fades away into the background and the only person who exists is the object of her affection, her groom. It is often difficult to get time with her without her beloved groom by her side. *"Love the Lord your God with all your heart and all your soul and all your mind."*

There are times when I look at Jamie and I am consumed with affection for her, where every part of my being feels in complete connection with every part of her being and I "feel" immense love for her. Sometimes I look at her and "feel," not just think, she is the coolest, most important person in the whole world. My whole heart and my entire soul and all of my mind is entirely focused on her and loves her completely. The entire world could burn down around us, and I would be OK because I'm with her.

This, I believe, is what being the Bride of Christ is. Guess what, I don't have times where I deny Christ and who He is. I don't have cycles in my Christian life that so many talk about having; having a close relationship with God one moment and the next moment feeling distant. I don't have times where I feel distant from Him and can't hear His voice. I don't have seasons where I lose sight of my calling. I don't believe I have seasons where my character is all over the place.

Every day my love for God is constant. Every day, all day long, I think about Him and am talking with Him. He is the only one that I always want to be with and talk to all the time. I'm certainly not perfect and would never claim to be. However, I have to say I have a fraction of the love for Him that Jamie does, but I love Him more and more every day. Every day I am growing deeper and deeper in *"Love the Lord your God with all your heart and all your soul and all your mind."*

What does that love look like from the outside? The greatest example I can think of from my life is Jamie. She has such great love for God the Father, the Son, and the Holy Spirit. You've seen it all over the pages of this book and the first Heaven's Chambers book. You can't talk to her without seeing it. Anywhere we go, and anyone we talk to, the first and most prominent thought she has is, "I have got to tell you about my groom. I have got to tell you about the love of my life. I have to tell you about my Jesus."

When Jamie and I go anywhere, it is always in the **back** of my mind that I will have an opportunity to tell someone about who God is, about how much He loves them, about what a great Comforter He is, about how He can heal and deliver them, about what He wants to do in their life. I am always willing to tell someone about God desiring to have a relationship with them. It is a rare day that I don't talk about my relationship with God to someone and encourage them toward having a relationship with Him and surrendering their whole life to Him.

For Jamie it's different. When she goes somewhere it's in the *front* of her mind, it's the first thing she thinks about. She thinks, "OK I'm going out into the world. I'm going to get into some good God trouble. Who can I encourage? Who can I tell about Jesus? Who can I heal? Who can I deliver from satan, the one who binds them in slavery to him? How can I stop the enemy on his quest to lie, steal, and kill?" The greatest event in the whole world to Jamie is when she has the opportunity to impart part of who she is in Christ, part of Christ Himself, into another individual. There is **NOTHING** she would rather talk about. There is no one she would rather be with than Him.

"The Spirit and the Bride say, "Come." And let the one who hears say, "Come." And let the one who is thirsty come; let the one who desires take the water of life without price." Revelation 22:17 (ESV) As the Bride we are to "take up" with the Spirit to call to those who

are thirsty, to call to those who desire to take the water of life within themselves. We put on the garments and jewels of a Bride and present ourselves to walk alongside the groom, to echo His call to those who need new life. Our whole beings should strive to put on the bright white garments of purity and love toward God. It's time to stop the self-centered thoughts of what God will do for us. What will you do to prepare to be spotless and blameless in His sight on that day?

"Blessed are those who wash their robes, so they may have the right to the tree of life and that they may enter the city by the gates." Revelation 22:14 (ESV)

"Let us rejoice and exult and give Him the glory, for the marriage of the Lamb has come, and the Bride has made herself ready; it was granted her to clothe herself with fine linen, bright and pure – for the fine linen is the righteous deeds of the saints." Revelation 19:7-8

Twenty-Nine

Your Chamber

You are Incredible. You are tremendously loved by the Father who designed you to love Him. You have a purpose to fulfill because He created you with purpose. Go up and into your chamber on purpose! You have everything to gain and absolutely nothing to lose. The time is now at hand to begin having your own countless chamber times in heaven. If I can do it, so can You!

Going up and into the chamber is a safe place for you because the Father has created this chamber place especially for you. It is a place to be with Jesus. It is a place where all of your New will begin and continue to be New every time you are there. You will be taken up and right into the chamber of His heart. He desires to spend time with You! His love for you and your love for him will increase. All of this love will over flow into you! Experiencing the chamber in Heaven is something you will not want to miss out on because it is a real place and you will be meeting with the real God. The time to begin is Now!

Simply find a comfortable place to be alone. Bring along your bible, paper and pen to write with so you can journal any words or experiences He gives you. Ask Jesus to help your thoughts to quiet down and think on him. Let the Holy Spirit know that you give Him permission to take you up and into your chamber. Relax in the Lord. He will always show up.

Let me explain to you what I experience each time I go up and in. When I am in my comfortable place, usually sitting on my bed with my bedroom door closed, I close my eyes and then I ask the Holy Spirit to take me up and into my chamber. I guess you could say I give the Holy Spirit permission to travel my spirit. God can travel our spirits without our permission if He chooses which I have experienced, but I like to be the one to ask. I feel my spirit going up and I see my portal as it begins to surround me. When I am surrounded by my portal, it looks like I am looking up inside of a tornado.

As I am traveling in my portal up to my chamber, I see an expansive, beautiful black canvas as far as my eye can see, similar to traveling through outer space. I see twinkling white lights, large globes of light, streams of lights or various shapes of white lights and all of them are alive with motion. Sometimes when I go up, I feel like I am still aware of my physical surroundings but most times my surroundings seem to disappear. But when I arrive, I know I am there in my chamber.

My chamber is too beautiful to describe. It always feels like the Holy Spirit has placed me in a room, inside a dwelling place, a place that is saturated with peace and love. I am usually standing in front of my chamber window while I wait for Jesus to come. It takes no time at all and Jesus will be standing next to me. I can always feel His love, His presence, and His peace. Frequently, I am able to see heaven which appears to look like a tremendous large planet. I often observe the activity in the throne room or other activities going on in Heaven.

I know that the chambers Jesus made for us to dwell in exist in the sky of heaven. They are built in the atmosphere of the Third Heaven and I am very aware of other peoples' chambers when I am there. I believe every one's chamber is uniquely designed by Jesus. All of creation was created by Jesus. God spoke and Jesus created. That to me is amazing! John 1:3 *"He* (Jesus) *created everything there is. Nothing exists that He didn't make."* God who sits upon His throne never stops creating something new for us to enjoy in heaven as well as on the earth. Our God is movable. He moves things into place for us, His children. I believe we should be His movable Brides. To be His united movable congregation speaking in His authority to move things out of our way. We move not backward but we move forward, depositing His love and glory power wherever we go.

Let's start moving!

"And each went straight forward; wherever the spirit would go, they went, without turning as they went." Ezekiel 1:12 (RSV)

www.ingramcontent.com/pod-product-compliance
Lightning Source LLC
Chambersburg PA
CBHW030919090426
42737CB00007B/249

Thirty

Declaration Chamber

I DECLARE IN THE NAME OF JESUS, GOD'S ONLY SON AND IN THE GLORY POWER OF HIS HOLY SPIRIT;

YOU WILL PROSPER, YOU WILL BE HEALED!

YOU WILL BE DELIVERED FROM THE EVIL ONE!

YOU WILL JUMP INTO HIS KINGDOM AGE ON THIS EARTH TO FULFILL YOUR PURPOSE!

HEAVEN AND EARTH WILL BECOME ONE IN YOUR LIFE!

YOU WILL ALLOW HIS GLORY TO FLOW FREELY THROUGH YOU, FLOWING OUT INTO THIS DARK WORLD, TO PULL DOWN STRONGHOLDS, TO EXPOSE ALL DARKNESS AND TO SET ALL THE CAPTIVES FREE!

YOU WILL RUN AND NOT GROW WEARY!

YOU WILL BE FILLED WITH SOUND WISDOM!

YOU WILL RISE UP AS A MIGHTY BRIDE OF CHRIST MOVING FORWARD IN HIS LOVE!

YOU WILL GO AND TAKE SPIRITUAL DOMINION OVER YOUR PROMISED LAND!

YOU WILL BE FEARLESS AND FILLED WITH THE STRENGTH OF THE LORD!

YOU WILL SEE THE REALM OF HEAVEN OPEN AS YOU GO UP AND INTO YOUR CHAMBER!

YOU WILL BE TRAINED BY THE LORD OUR GOD!

YOU WILL BE FILLED WITH THE FRUITS AND THE GIFTS OF THE SPIRIT!

YOU WILL LIVE IN UNITY WITH YOUR BROTHERS AND YOUR SISTERS!

YOU WILL SUCCEED!!!

****

We the Brides of Christ will strategically use our weapons of warfare and the enemy will never get his hands on us. Instead, we will get our hands on him and cast him out and back into his chamber of fire.

"It is for Freedom that Christ has set us Free. Stand firm, then, and do not let yourselves be burdened again by a yoke of slavery," Galatians 5:1 (NIV)

Ascending up and into our heavenly chambers is a spiritual place to be in the presence of the Father, Son and the Holy Spirit. They will fill us with their glory and we will be ignited with the Fire Love of God's eternal flames which will burn forever inside the chambers of our Hearts! Then we can go out and break into the lives of people on the earth who are in a chamber of slavery, bound by chains and waiting to be set FREE!

Love Jamie

"God raised us up and seated us with Him in the Heavenly realms in Jesus Christ." Ephesians 2:6(NIV)